D0122160

THE DARK SIDE OF ISLAM

**OTHER CROSSWAY BOOKS
by R. C. Sproul**
The Consequences of Ideas
Defending Your Faith
Justified by Faith Alone
Saved from What?
The Spirit of Revival (with Archie Parrish)
When Worlds Collide

THE DARK SIDE OF ISLAM

R. C. SPROUL
AND
ABDUL SALEEB

CROSSWAY BOOKS

A DIVISION OF
GOOD NEWS PUBLISHERS
WHEATON, ILLINOIS

The Dark Side of Islam

Copyright © 2003 by R. C. Sproul

Published by Crossway Books
        a division of Good News Publishers
        1300 Crescent Street
        Wheaton, Illinois 60187.

All rights reserved. No part of this publication may be reproduced, stored in a retrieval system, or transmitted in any form by any means, electronic, mechanical, photocopy, recording, or otherwise, without the prior permission of the publisher, except as provided by USA copyright law.

Cover design: Kirk DouPonce, UDG / DesignWorks, Sisters, Oregon

Cover photo: Richard T. Nowitz, National Geographic

First printing 2003

Printed in the United States of America

Scripture references are from the *New King James Version*. Copyright © 1982, Thomas Nelson, Inc. Used by permission.

Library of Congress Cataloging-in-Publication Data
Sproul, R. C. (Robert Charles), 1939-
   The dark side of Islam / R.C. Sproul and Abdul Saleeb.
     p. cm.
   Includes bibliographical references and index.
   ISBN 1-58134-441-4
    1. Islam—Controversial literature. 2. Islam—Relations—
Christianity. 3. Christianity and other religions—Islam. I. Saleeb,
Abdul. II. Title.
BT1170.S67   2003
297—dc21   2003004798

LB		13	12	11	10	09	08	07	06	05	04	03
15	14	13	12	11	10	9	8	7	6	5	4	3	2

CONTENTS

INTRODUCTION

R. C. Sproul: Since the events of September 11 and the beginning of America's war on terrorism, there has been an unprecedented interest in the theological tenets of Islam as well as sincere questions about the true nature of this faith that has taken on such violent overtones in the minds of many. This book is based on a series of conversations with my friend Abdul Saleeb (his pseudonym). In the first seven chapters we discuss the theological points of issue and of conflict between various manifestations of Islam and Christianity. In the final chapter, Saleeb offers his own perspective on the "dark side" of Islam.

Abdul was reared in the Muslim faith in a Muslim country, was converted to Christianity, and has studied thoroughly both Islam and Christianity. He has a degree in Christian theology and is the coauthor of *Answering Islam,* written with Norman Geisler.[1]

Abdul Saleeb: I am very glad to finally see among Christians today an interest in understanding Islam. It is very important for the Christian church to know the challenge of Islam and how to respond to it. There are 5 to 7 million Muslims living in America. Many Christians interact with Muslims every day—as colleagues, coworkers, neighbors. Thus, it is very important for every Christian to have a better understanding of Islam, what Muslims believe, and how to respond to the typical Muslim's questions about the Christian faith.

It is also important not to stereotype Islam as a simple religion that promotes violence. That is not at all the case. In fact, Islam has a rich tradition in its intellectual history and in its cultural achievements. Throughout history, the Muslim world has produced many philosophers and scientists. We must take Islam seriously as a coherent, systematic faith that presents strong challenges against the Christian faith. After years of studying Islam, living and practicing it, and coauthoring a book on it, I have boiled down the fundamental differences between Islam and Christianity to four main areas: 1) the nature and the authority of the Bible, 2) the nature of God, 3) the view of humankind, and 4) the view of Christ. I hope that at least one thing will become clear in our conversations: Islam and Christianity have diametrically opposed ideas on these four important subjects.

Under each of these main headings we will discuss two subpoints. When we discuss Scripture (chapter 1), we will see that Muslims reject the authenticity of our Bible and therefore reject its authority.

When we discuss God, we will first talk about the Islamic rejection of the idea of the fatherhood of God (chapter 2). It is a great privilege as Christians that we can call God our heavenly Father. In fact, that is how Jesus taught us to pray. The intimacy we can have with God as His children through faith in Jesus Christ is good news to us; however, when Muslims hear us referring to God as our Father or referring to ourselves as children of God, it does not sound like good news at all to them. We need to put ourselves in the shoes of Muslims and try to understand what they feel and think when they hear Christian terminology. Also and more importantly, Islam very strongly rejects any notion of the Trinity (chapter 3).

In our discussion of humankind we will address the Christian understanding of sin (chapter 4), including the doctrine of original sin, and the Christian understanding of salvation (chapter 5), both of which Islam rejects. How is humankind saved? How can we have a relationship with God? We will see that Islam and Christianity offer two radically different versions of how we can approach God.

Regarding our belief about Jesus Christ, we will talk about the Islamic denial of His death on the cross (chapter 6). Islam and the Qur'an very clearly reject Jesus' crucifixion. We will also discuss the Islamic denial of the deity of Jesus Christ (chapter 7).

Before we get into the details of this outline, let's discuss how the theological challenges that Islam presents to the Christian faith are coming not only from Muslims. In recent centuries, Western intellectuals, liberal Christian scholars, and Enlightenment thinkers have basically expressed the very same challenges to Christianity that Muslims have expressed for the past fourteen hundred years. It is understandable how Muslims can feel intellectually justified in rejecting Christianity. They might say, "We've been saying these things against Christianity for fourteen hundred years, and now your own Western scholars and your own Christian writers are saying the same things that we have been saying."

For example, the philosopher Immanuel Kant said this about the doctrine of the Trinity: "The doctrine of the Trinity provides nothing, absolutely nothing, of practical value even if one claims to understand it; still less when one is convinced that it far surpasses our understanding. It costs the student nothing to accept that we adore three or ten persons in the divinity. . . . Furthermore, this distinction offers absolutely no guidance for his conduct."[2]

Thomas Jefferson wrote this about the Christian doctrine of the Trinity: "When we shall have done away with the incomprehensible jargon of the Trinitarian arithmetic, that three are one, and one is three; when we shall have knocked down the artificial scaffolding, reared to mask from the view the very simple structure of Jesus; when, in short, we shall have unlearned everything which has been taught since his day, and got back to the pure and simple doctrines inculcated, we shall then be truly and worthily his disciples."[3] And a Muslim would say "Amen and amen" to Thomas Jefferson.

Dorothy Sayers, a Christian, wrote the following tongue-in-cheek play on the Athanasian Creed: "The Father is incomprehensible, the Son is incomprehensible, and the whole thing is incomprehensible. Trinity is something put in by theologians to make it more difficult—nothing to do with daily life or ethics."[4]

This is the impression many Westerners have had about the doctrine of the Trinity. A Muslim might say, "Our holy book, the Qur'an, told us fourteen hundred years ago that there is only one God, and we should worship that God; and that Christians have been misled from the teachings of Prophet Jesus when they have professed the doctrine of the Trinity. And now, after all these centuries, your own Western intellectuals and your own Christian scholars are rejecting such notions."

Another fundamental conviction of the Christian faith is that we are born in a state of sin, that Adam's sin has affected us. However, many surveys indicate that the vast majority of Americans—including evangelical Christians—believe that we are basically good people. Not many people adhere to the notion that somehow sin is deeply rooted within our very nature from the time of our conception. A Muslim might respond by saying, "We've been saying for all these years that humankind is basically good, and now Western people— including Christians—are coming to the same conclusions."

Also, the Christian faith believes that it is only because of Jesus' death on the cross that we can have any hope of salvation—our sins have been imputed to Him, and His righteousness has been imputed to us. Islam, on the other hand, claims that all people are responsible for their own actions and for their own salvation. Nobody else can pay for someone's sin. Theologian C. Stephen Evans wrote a book several years ago called *The Historical Christ and the Jesus of Faith* that traces the Enlightenment rejection of orthodox Christianity. He entitles one of the factors in this rejection "Moral Difficulties with the Atonement." He writes, "Theories of atonement, however, especially the popular forms of 'substitutionary' atonement, rather than being the solution, are often seen as part of the problem. The idea that God forgives human sin by virtue of punishing an innocent figure in our place raises a host of moral difficulties. The Enlightenment emphasized a view of individuals as morally autonomous agents; I am responsible only for my own choices. Such a moral perspective poses many questions for theories of atonement: Why must God punish at all? If punishment is indeed necessary, how can guilt be transferred to someone else? How can the suffering of an innocent person take away my guilt?"[5]

Once again a Muslim would say, "That's exactly what we've been saying for fourteen hundred years. It makes no sense that somebody else could take the punishment for my sins. I am responsible only for my own actions." Islam in this regard fits very well the thinking of modern Enlightenment people who believe that we are all responsible for ourselves.

Islam has a great appeal to people of all backgrounds because it presents itself as a very rational, intellectual, easy-to-understand faith. Muslims believe Christianity is filled with mysteries and mumbo jumbo that nobody can understand—people simply have to take all of it by faith. But Islam presents itself as a very rational, simple religion—the religion of nature that any child can understand.

In a seminary course I recently taught, I asked the students, "Will somebody explain to me what the doctrine of the Trinity is?" At first not a single person answered. Finally, a woman raised her hand with fear and trembling and said, "Well, the doctrine of the Trinity means that there are three parts in God."

I said, "Unfortunately, that's what many people think. But that understanding is ancient heresy." Many Christians do not understand the basics of their own faith; they can hardly explain it to others or defend it against somebody who challenges them. And the challenges do not just come from Muslims. The challenges come from people all around us: agnostics, rationalists, Enlightenment thinkers, postmodernists, and Muslims.

Islam also challenges the orthodox Christian view of Jesus Christ. At Easter 1996, *Time Magazine, U.S. World and News Report,* and *Newsweek* all had the same cover story: Jesus Christ. The *U.S. News* cover read: "In search of Jesus: who was he? New appraisals of his life and its meaning." *Newsweek's* cover: "Rethinking the resurrection—a new debate about the risen Christ." And *Time's* cover: "The search for Jesus. Some scholars are debunking the Gospels. Now traditionalists are fighting back. What are Christians to believe?"[6] Many of the articles refer to the Jesus Seminar and other liberal Christian scholars who deny all the fundamentals of the Christian faith with respect to the deity of Christ, His salvific work, and so on.

A Muslim might say, "The Qur'an, God's word to us fourteen hundred years ago, set the record straight. Your own Christian theologians and scholars and pastors and bishops are just now finding out that Jesus never claimed to be divine. He never said the things that you say He said." The Muslim might go on to say, "We didn't start the Jesus Seminar, for example. We didn't start liberal seminaries. Your own conclusions and research have led to what we have been saying all along—that Jesus was not God incarnate, and that many other things that orthodox Christianity has said about Christ are also untrue."

Once again, a Muslim would feel intellectually justified in

rejecting the Gospel. As Christians witness to Muslims, the defensive walls often go up. They say, "No thank you. What you are saying is not true. You had better read your own Christian scholars and see what they are saying."

The orthodox Christian view of the Bible is under attack from Western scholars. As the *Time* headline noted, "Some scholars are debunking the Gospels." A Muslim might say, "Your own scholars are saying that the Bible has been corrupted." Most professors in major American universities believe that the Bible had many hands involved in editing and revising it, putting it together to promote a particular agenda and point of view. Some Muslims see this as supporting their view that both the Old and the New Testaments have been corrupted. Members of the Jesus Seminar vote on the supposed authenticity of Jesus' sayings. I heard that there was only one sentence in the entire Gospel of John that they could agree was actually said by Christ. Everything else in John that was attributed to Christ was supposedly added later. A Muslim might say, "Even Christian scholars say that your Bible has been tampered with. It is no longer the pure Word of God, as the Qur'an is. And therefore, you should no longer believe it."

Thus, Islam challenges the Christian view of the Bible, of God, of humankind, and of Christ. It is crucial for Christians to know what we believe and why we believe it. You may never meet a Muslim, but these questions and these issues are raised not just by Muslims but by many people from different walks of life. As Christians we need to be better equipped to explain and defend our own faith.

1

ISLAM AND CHRISTIANITY
ON SCRIPTURE

Saleeb: The Muslim viewpoint on scripture is this: because man is prone to being led astray, God has sent prophets throughout history, and these prophets have brought revelations from God. According to Islamic belief, all revelations from God previous to the Qur'an have been either lost or tampered with and corrupted. Thus they are no longer authentic or reliable and therefore no longer authoritative.

The Qur'an, according to Muslims, is God's final word to humanity and is the only authentic, authoritative, and reliable information from God because it is the only information that has not been tampered with and corrupted.

However, the situation is not quite this simple. Although this Islamic view is what Muslim theologians and apologists claim, the Qur'an itself gives us a very different picture. In fact, the Qur'an has many complimentary things to say about the previous Scriptures. Sura (chapter) 5:44, for example, says, "It was We [Allah] who revealed the Law to Moses: therein was guidance and light."[1] It goes on to say, "And in their footsteps We sent Jesus the son of Mary, confirming the Law that had come before him. We sent him the Gospel: therein was guidance and light" (v. 46). My favorite verse in the whole Qur'an is Sura 5:68: "Say, O People of the Book! [Jews and Christians] Ye have no ground to stand upon unless you stand fast by the Law, the Gospel, and all the revelation that has come to you from your Lord."

In the Qur'an Allah tells Muhammad, "If thou wert in doubt as to what We have revealed unto thee, then ask those who have been reading the Book from before thee" (Sura 10:94). Sura 29:46 says, "And dispute ye not with the People of the Book, except with means better." Later in that verse we read, "But say [to the People of the Book], 'We believe in the Revelation [the Qur'an] which has come down to us and in that which came down to you. Our God and your God is one; and it is to Him we bow (in Islam).'"

Muhammad very much wanted to say to the Jews and Christians, "Listen, I am a monotheist. I am a prophet like Moses and Jesus. We are all alike. We worship the same God. My Qur'an is basically in confirmation of the previous Scriptures. We all agree on the essentials. The Qur'an is the final word from God, but the Law and the Gospel were also guidance and light and revelation and mercy from God to humanity." However, since Muhammad himself was not very well educated, he did not have firsthand knowledge about the Christian and the Jewish Scriptures. Later in Islamic history, as Muslims came into contact with Jewish and Christian communities and began to read the Bible, they realized that the Old and New Testaments contradict the Qur'an on very serious issues.

So Muslims had to come up with a theory to explain this situation. On the one hand, the Qur'an says that the previous Scriptures are the Word of God, and, according to the Qur'an, "No one can change the Word of God." On the other hand, the Scriptures from the Christians and Jews do not agree with the teachings of the Qur'an. What is the solution? The doctrine of *tahrif,* the Arabic word for corruption, claims that the Jews and Christians have corrupted their Scriptures, and that is why their Bible no longer agrees with the teachings of the Qur'an. And some Muslims say, "Your own scholars say the same thing: that Moses didn't write the Torah, that Jesus didn't say these things. These were all fabricated and put in the mouths of people like Christ and other folks."

Sproul: You once mentioned to me that the Qur'an speaks of Jesus' virgin birth, that Muhammad had talked about Christ's miracles, and about His being a wonderful prophet. I asked you, "Where did Muhammad get that information?" Your response was that Muslims believe Muhammad was getting separate, independent, divine revelation about these facts of Jesus' life.

But that is really not much evidence for the inspiration of Muhammad as a prophet—for him to be able to talk about information that was available long before he lived. Usually what authenticates a prophet is when he gives vivid descriptions of things that don't happen until long after he has prophesied them. One of the most astonishing things about the Bible—

this Bible that is supposedly so "corrupt"—is that, centuries before certain events take place, they are predicted, and then they are fulfilled with uncanny accuracy. Some people have calculated the odds against these prophecies being fulfilled fortuitously as being virtually astronomical. One of the strongest arguments for the authenticity of the Bible is the multitude of passages where detailed events that have not yet taken place are predicted—not vague, studied ambiguities about the future, but specific events—and then these predicted events come to pass. A striking example is Jesus' prediction of the destruction of Jerusalem and the dispersion of the Jews (Matthew 24). Nobody in Jesus' day thought this was even remotely possible, yet He gave a detailed prophecy that was indeed fulfilled.

This is why nineteenth-century critics coming out of the Enlightenment, who wanted to discredit the authority of Scripture, attacked predictive prophecy. Their working assumption was that anytime a passage in Scripture seemed to demonstrate the fulfillment of a prophecy, the only way to account for that from a naturalistic perspective was to assume that the text had been written after the fact.

At the turn of the twentieth century, higher critical scholars were somewhat boastful about the so-called assured results of higher criticism, including the conviction that the Gospel of John wasn't written until the middle of the second century. However, I don't know any respectable scholar who would argue that today. If you look at the list of so-called assured results at the turn of the twentieth century and compare them to current criticism, you see the egg all over the faces of the critical scholars who were trying to undermine the authority of the Scripture. They were fighting the contest of naturalism against supernaturalism.

What nineteenth-century liberal Christianity sought to achieve was the revision of Christianity, in fact, the capture of Christianity from its historic significance by repudiating all supernatural elements of the biblical narrative and then salvaging from that a core of ethics that could be preserved to keep the church going. Emil Brunner, the Swiss scholar, wrote a book in the early twentieth century called *Der Mittler*,[2] in which he observed that the whole effort of nineteenth-century criticism, predominantly German scholarship, was a monument to unbelief. Because their guns were aimed constantly at the Scriptures, those nineteenth-century critics should not be classified as orthodox Christians.

Two of the main targets were the Old Testament and, of course, the Torah, which is so important not only to Christianity but also to Judaism and historically to the Muslim faith. Even though Muhammad didn't know all of its contents, he endorsed it. Thus, three of the great religions had a high view of the Torah. Then came the Graf-Wellhausen theory of the nineteenth century that the Torah was corrupted— that it was written, initially at least, by four different writers, or, according to redaction criticism, edited by four redactors. These critics theorized four sources, J, E, D, and P. The J stands for the Yahweh source, the one who refers to God in the Torah by the name Yahweh. The writer/redactor who refers to God as Elohim is the E source. D is the Deuteronomic source, as in Deuteronomy. P is the priestly source. These critics claim that, long after the patriarchal period, when the priestly caste emerged and were trying to dignify their political authority by showing their divinely ordained position, they read back into the Torah certain activities that would have given divine sanction to their privileged positions. This view implies not only corruption of the text but also the corruption of the people involved in it. This theory then became even more refined, claiming that there were not only four editors, but four of each—J1, J2, J3, J4; E1, E2, and so forth—and thus sixteen redactors.

William Foxwell Albright, acknowledged as the dean of archeological experts in the twentieth century, became disgusted with where this kind of scholarship was headed. He wrote that these biblical critics ignore the most important criteria for historiography, which is the empirical data of history, and that their interpretation was being completely controlled by secular philosophies. He noted particularly the influence of nineteenth-century Hegelian philosophy. The major buzzword in nineteenth-century philosophy was *evolution;* the assumption of evolutionary philosophy was that everything in this world—not just biology, but all institutions, economics, psychology—goes through a process of evolutionary development from the simple to the complex.

These philosophers looked around the rest of the world, outside of Judeo-Christianity, and saw that in antiquity virtually all religions were either animistic or polytheistic. They looked at the notable exception of Judaism, with its ancient Torah affirming monotheism on its first page, and thought, "Wait a minute. This doesn't fit the pattern of evolutionary history. Judaism must be like every other religion, going through a gradual stage of development from animism to polytheism to henotheism and finally to monotheism." Some of the radical critics thought that monotheism came as late as the post-exilic period. Others thought it might have come as early as the eighth-century prophets. However, none of these critics thought there was monotheism in the days of Moses, or in the Torah.

And yet the Torah unambiguously attests to monotheism, so what do you assume if you're an evolutionary naturalist? Hegelian philosophy assumed that the monotheism could not have been in the original text; it had to have been written back into the text. Monotheism in the time of the Torah would break the mold of natural evolutionary development, which, they believed, applies to all religions as well as to biological organisms. Thus, the theory of biblical literature was determined by a naturalistic philosophy whose worldview was already completely antithetical to the biblical worldview.

Saleeb: And given those assumptions, as you pointed out earlier, Islam itself would be proved false because the Qur'an says that God gave Moses the Torah and monotheism. Muslims like to quote the arguments of critical scholars against the Bible, but they don't understand that, if these arguments are carried to their logical conclusion, they also cast doubt on the Qur'an.

Sproul: The Jesus Seminar offers a contemporary example of criticism that attacks the Bible. It is what I would call the "journalistic phase of theology." In other words, the more bizarre the theory is, the more attention it gets in the media. In theology no less than in politics there is a spectrum of beliefs. We talk about the right and the left, conservatives and liberals, a radical right and a radical left. At the extreme ends of the continuum are the lunatic fringes. In my judgment the Jesus Seminar represents the lunatic fringe of the radical left of biblical criticism. I don't take them seriously. Their scholarship is pseudo-scholarship. Not even the higher critics of the nineteenth and the twentieth centuries—including Bultmann on his worst day—ever went as far as the Jesus Seminar does in its rejection of biblical authenticity with its scissors-and-paste methodology of cutting out verses from the Scriptures. The early church heretic Marcion, in his madness, never dreamed of going to the extremes that the members of the Jesus Seminar do. They represent a tiny blip on the radar of historical scholarship, a blip of radical extremism; and they have not, in my judgment, demonstrated enough sober scholarship to warrant giving them much attention.

The Jesus Seminar members adopt naturalistic philosophical assumptions that rule out miracles. The agenda of the nineteenth-century liberals was to get rid of all the miracles, all the supernatural. One of their targets was the virgin birth. It went against normal biological propagation, so they tried to deny that it had occurred. They first reinterpreted the biblical notion of "virgin" (e.g., Isa. 7:14), reducing its meaning to "young woman." In so doing they showed utter disregard for the immediate context of the birth narratives. Many of them tried to say, "We believe in Jesus; we just don't believe in the virgin birth."

The Jesus Seminar argues that Jesus was not even born in Bethlehem. Why are they so eager to claim this? There's a simple reason. An Old Testament prophecy predicted that this tiny little village six miles south of Jerusalem would be the birthplace of the Messiah; if they agree that Jesus was born in Bethlehem, they would have a problem of *vaticinia ex eventu,* that is, trying to explain a predictive prophecy by saying it had to have been written after the fact. Their scholarship is simply dishonest.

I have had to wrestle with these attacks on the authority of Scripture for forty years. And yet I think there is less reason today than at any time in church history to be skeptical about the veracity and integrity of the biblical witness. No book has been subjected to more rigorous scrutiny, more vicious attacks. Abraham Kuyper, a Christian who became prime minister of the Netherlands in 1900 and who founded the Free University of Amsterdam, said that nineteenth-century criticism degenerated into vandalism because it was an all-out attack with no holds barred, and sober scholarship was left in the wake. However, if we look clearly at the historical record and at the attempts to discredit it, no document from antiquity has been manifested more frequently to have authenticity than the Bible, particularly the New Testament.

Saleeb: And because it is authentic and originally from God, it is therefore authoritative. It has not been surpassed by the Qur'an.

2

Islam and Christianity on the Fatherhood of God

Saleeb: Another of the most important concepts in the Christian faith is the fatherhood of God. Jesus taught us in the Lord's Prayer to address God as "our Father in heaven" (Matt. 6:9). We Christians feel privileged to be able to talk to God in such intimate terms. And we believe that through faith in Christ we can become adopted children of God. When Christians talk about this to Muslims, they think that they are sharing good news. Christians don't understand that to Muslim ears, that sounds like horrible news. To them it sounds blasphemous to think of God as our Father and us as His children.

As Christians, again, we need to understand that since both Islam and Christianity are monotheistic faiths, there are many things we do hold in common. Christians and Muslims believe that God is one, that God is just, that God is sovereign, that God rules, that God forgives. God has sent prophets and has sent revelations. There are many areas of agreement, but we cannot ignore the fact that there are very fundamental differences also.

Following is a sura of the Qur'an. Sura 112 is recited in prayer every day by millions of Muslims around the world. It is an essential part of the daily prayers of a Muslim: "Say He is Allah, the One and Only; Allah the Eternal, Absolute; He begetteth not, nor is He begotten; and there is none like unto Him."

Islam heavily emphasizes the absolute sovereignty of God: "It is not befitting (to the majesty of) Allah that He should beget a son. Glory be to Him! When He determines a matter, He only says to it, 'Be,' and it is" (Sura 19:35). Abdullah Yusuf Ali, translator of the edition of the Qur'an from which this book is quoting, says this in a footnote to this verse: "Begetting a son is a physical act depending on the needs of men's animal nature. Allah Most High is independent of all needs, and it is derogatory to Him to attribute such an act to Him. It is merely a relic of pagan and anthropomorphic materialist superstitions."[1]

This belief goes back to the Qur'an itself—that to talk about God as our Father implies sexual relations, and attributes something that is not right to God: "To him [Allah] is due the primal origin of the heavens and the earth: How can He have a son when He hath no consort? He created all things, and He hath full knowledge of all things" (Sura 6:101).

Sura 2:116 reads, "They say, 'Allah hath begotten a son': Glory be to Him—Nay, to Him belongs all that is in the heavens and on earth: everything renders worship to Him." In his footnote on this verse Yusuf Ali says, "It is a derogation from the glory of Allah—in fact it is blasphemy—to say that Allah begets sons like a man or an animal."[2] And of course, as Christians we say, "That's not what Christians believe. We are not attributing a sexual act to God when we talk about the fatherhood of God or that we are sons of God." But that's not how a Muslim understands it. Yusuf Ali goes on to say, "The Christian doctrine is here emphatically repudiated. If words have any meaning, it would mean an attribution to Allah of a material nature, and of the lower animal functions of sex."[3] Thus, to Muslims it sounds like blasphemy to call God, with such intimacy, "our heavenly Father."

And I'm just using the word *Father,* but there is a plethora of other images in the Bible about God: as a shepherd who carries the sheep in His arms, and as a wounded husband who goes after His unfaithful wife, the nation of Israel. Christ is viewed as the bridegroom coming for His church, the bride. We have many tender images of God and His relationship to humanity. But the dominant Qur'anic and Islamic image of God is that of a master, and our relationship with Him is that of a servant to a master. Islam does not allow for any intimacy between humanity and God or for us to call God "our heavenly Father." As Christians we need to be informed about the Muslim mindset and what they hear when they hear phrases like *heavenly Father* or *Son of God.*

Sproul: First of all, as you've indicated, orthodox Christianity would agree with virtually every one of those texts in terms of a complete repudiation of any kind of crass idea of divine physical propagation of children like we find in Greek and Roman mythology. The idea of gods sexually interacting with human beings is utterly foreign to Judeo-Christianity as it would be to Islam.

Obviously, when Christianity speaks of the fatherhood of God, the Son of God, and the children of God, it does not mean to communicate this idea of physical, biological propagation. Although that has arisen in certain cults, it has been completely rejected by virtually every Christian denomination, liberal or conservative. Also, the rejection of the idea of the fatherhood of God is one place where the Muslim scholarly community cannot appeal to the liberal element of Western Christianity for support. The discipline or science of comparative religion originated in the nineteenth century. As the world became smaller through modern forms of travel, and people began to interact with other cultures, the whole science of comparative religion developed, seeking to discern the points of commonality that linked Judaism, Hinduism, Buddhism, Confucianism, Taoism, Islam, Christianity, and other religions. In German scholarship, among those who were introducing this science of comparative religion, the quest was for the so-called *Wesen,* the essence or being of religion—the basic stuff that is true of all religions. One of the most significant academicians of that era was the church historian and theologian Adolf von Harnack, who wrote one of the most definitive studies of the history of Christian dogma. He also wrote a small monograph entitled *What Is Christianity?* Looking for the *Wesen,* the "is-ness," the stuff of which Christianity is made, he basically reduced the essence of the Christian religion to two basic premises—the universal fatherhood of God and the universal brotherhood of man—saying that these constituted the basic message of the Christian faith. I'm convinced that the New Testament doesn't teach either of those premises.

We need to look carefully at how the Old and particularly the New Testament articulate their understanding of the fatherhood of God and the so-called brotherhood of man. An important twentieth-century scholar, Joachim Jeremias, studied the fatherhood of God. He looked through all of the literature—not only the Old Testament but the Talmudic writings, the Rabbinic writings, and every extant Jewish text that survives to the twentieth century—to examine how within Judaism the title *Father* was attributed to God. Nowhere in the Old Testament or in any of the Rabbinic writings could he find a Jewish person addressing God in prayer directly as Father. This seems to parallel the absence of intimacy pointed to by Muslim scholars.

In fact, Jeremias concluded that the earliest example of a Jewish person addressing God directly as "Father" is in the tenth century A.D. (However, in every prayer of Jesus of Nazareth recorded in the New Testament, with one exception, Jesus addressed God as Father.) Jeremias wrote that the Jewish people had a list of proscribed and acceptable titles that could be used in worship and in private prayer that would not be in any way denigrating to the glory and majesty of God. Conspicuously absent from that list was the title *Father*. On rare occasions God was referred to indirectly as the father of the human race, only insofar as He was its creator, but not in the crass way to which the Muslims object or in the way that Christians understand God's fatherhood.

Jeremias's thesis was that we in the Christian community today routinely address God as Father. The Lord's Prayer is an integral part of our corporate worship. And if you listen to a group of Christians praying, inevitably the most common form of address you will hear from their lips as they pray is "Father." And yet, because it is so predominant in Christian culture, we often take this for granted. Jeremias was claiming that in Jesus' day, His calling God "Father" was a radical departure from Jewish tradition. The significance of this radical innovation was noted by His contemporaries. In fact, it infuriated His enemies, that He would have the audacity to suggest that He had this kind of intimate relationship with God.

Further, in the New Testament that relationship is seen from the other perspective. God is heard speaking from heaven declaring, "This is My beloved Son in whom I am well pleased" (Matt. 17:5). And Jesus bears the title "Son of God," although in a very carefully guarded way. When Christ is called the Son of God, He is called the *monogeneis*—the only begotten of the Father. The church understood very early that this did not mean He had a beginning in time. There wasn't any idea of the Father's procreating or siring a son.

When the Bible speaks in terms of sonship, it refers not only to biological generation: it also speaks regularly of sonship as a description of a relationship of obedience. When Jesus talked about setting people free, the Pharisees became upset, saying, "We are Abraham's descendants, and have never been in bondage to anyone" (John 8:33). Jesus replied, "If you were Abraham's children, you would do the works of Abraham" (v. 39). To be called a child of God meant to be one who obeyed God. Sonship here was defined not in biological terms but in ethical terms. And in that sense the New Testament speaks of Christ's unique relationship as the One who is perfectly obedient to the Father.

But Jesus then tells His disciples to pray, "Our Father in heaven . . ." (Matt. 6:9). That was radical. That was astonishing, initially, to those who heard it. It doesn't surprise me at all that Muslims would be offended by that. Orthodox Jews would also be offended, because it was a serious departure from their tradition. In fact, from the Fall throughout the Old Testament there is a history of the wall separating humankind from God because of sin. An angel with a flaming sword guarded the entrance to paradise (Gen. 3:24) to prevent us from having an intimate relationship with God.

In Romans 8 Paul writes about the concept of our adoption by God the Father by virtue of the work of the Holy Spirit, who gives us now, as we are adopted into the family of God, the right and the authority to say, "Abba, Father" (v. 15). We now have the right to address God as Father; the relationship of estrangement that defined our relationship prior to the work of Christ and the atonement is now ended; the wall has been removed. God has been so gracious that He has not only forgiven us of our sins but has invited us into the intimate fellowship of being family members. Even though we are not His children by nature, we are His children by adoption; by virtue of our relationship to Christ, we are now included in the family of God.

One of the most moving stories in the Old Testament is the story of Jonathan's son Mephibosheth, who was lame in both legs (2 Samuel 9). When the news came that Saul and Jonathan had been killed, some men in David's camp wanted to kill all of the survivors from Saul's family, lest any would try to seize power from David and keep him from rising to kingship. David was upset about the proposed purge. He asked if there was anybody left from the house of Saul so that he could honor him in memory of his love for Jonathan. David's men found Jonathan's lame son, who had been secreted away, and brought him to David. Mephibosheth was terrified. He assumed that he was being delivered for execution. Instead David said that as long as Mephibosheth was alive, he would eat at the king's table and would be regarded as a member of the king's family. This is what happens when we come to the Lord's Table; we come as God's children. Because of the love of the Father for the Son, and our adoption, we can have this filial relationship.

This relationship differs markedly from any found in Islam. This is one of the ways in which Islam is so profoundly impoverished; it doesn't have an avenue for us to be restored to that filial relationship, to that relationship of intimacy, for which we were created in the first place. This concept of adoption is vital to our whole understanding of redemption, something we must not take for granted. When John writes about this in 1 John, he introduces the statement with the word *behold*. That's like a sign at a railroad crossing with a flashing red light: stop, look, and listen. Hold it right there, pay attention. Something important is coming. "Behold what manner of love the Father has bestowed on us, that we should be called children of God!" (1 John 3:1). Even the apostles in the first century were overwhelmed with amazement that the status of a filial relationship to God would be accorded to us because of the work of Christ.

Saleeb: As we talk with Muslims about the fatherhood of God, it is important to know and emphasize the fact that we're not talking about physical procreation on the part of God. And an emphasis on the aspect of obedience as a definition of sonship is very important. We also need to understand that when Islam came on the scene, it was in the context of paganism. So in fact the Qur'an originally was denouncing the pagan views of the fatherhood of God and of humans being His children. Islam arose in that context, but later Islamic theology simply took off from there and never developed humankind's relationship with God in terms of intimacy and relationship.

Fuller Seminary recently conducted a survey of six hundred former Muslims who had become Christians. One of the factors involved in the conversions of these former Muslims was the emphasis on the love of God and the intimacy that believers can have with God as their heavenly Father. This was an important factor in drawing these former Muslims to Christ. We need to present this truth to all Muslim people.

ISLAM AND CHRISTIANITY ON THE TRINITY

Sproul: We have looked at the objection Muslims have to the Christian understanding of the fatherhood of God and our being called the children of God. Another major stumbling block Muslims have regarding Christians' view of God has to do with the Trinity.

Saleeb: Muslims believe that the essence of knowledge is the fact that there is one God and one God alone. In fact, the Qur'an is filled with passages that talk about the sovereignty, majesty, and absolute transcendence of God. Basically, Muslims believe that God has sent prophets to all humanity. They have all brought the same message: that there is one true God, and we need to worship and obey Him. But all other religions have gotten off track. Islam is the final religion of God to humanity and the gift of Islam is to restore pure monotheism to the world. Muslims believe Christianity has been profoundly corrupted by the notion of the Trinity. To Muslim ears, it sounds very much like we are compromising the unity and oneness of God, that we are introducing a plurality, a compound-ness, into the being and nature of God.

Only two verses in the entire Qur'an specifically refer to the doctrine of the Trinity. One is Sura 4:171: "O people of the book! [Jews and Christians] Commit no excesses in your religion: nor say of Allah aught but the truth. Christ Jesus the son of Mary was (no more than) a messenger of Allah, and His Word, which He bestowed on Mary." The verse goes on to say, "Say not 'Trinity': desist: it will be better for you: for Allah is One God: glory be to Him."

The other passage is Sura 5:73: "They do blaspheme who say: Allah is one of three in a Trinity: for there is no God except One God. If they desist not from their word (of blasphemy), verily, a grievous penalty will befall the blasphemers among them." Sura 5:116-117 relates a conversation that is supposed to take place between Jesus and God on the day of judgment: "And behold! Allah will say: 'O Jesus the son of Mary! Didst thou say unto men, "Worship me and my mother as gods in derogation of Allah"?' He [Jesus] will say, 'Glory to Thee! Never could I say what I had no right (to say). Had I said such a thing, Thou wouldst indeed have known it. Thou knowest what is in my heart, though I know not what is in Thine. . . . Never said I to them aught except what Thou didst command me to say, to wit, "Worship Allah—my Lord and your Lord."'"

Based on this passage, some people believe that Muhammad profoundly misunderstood the Christian doctrine of the Trinity, and that early Muslims thought of the Trinity as the Father, Mary, and Jesus. We won't examine these misunderstandings in any further detail. The bottom line is that, based on these Qur'anic passages and on the fundamental notion that there is one God, Muslims have denied the doctrine of the Trinity. They accuse Christians of committing blasphemy by claiming that there is more to that oneness of God. Christians are also accused of committing a logical fallacy; according to Muslims, the doctrine of the Trinity is an incoherent, illogical notion that many Christians themselves don't understand and often cannot explain or defend to an outsider.

Shabbir Akhtar is a Muslim theologian who studied at Cambridge. I commend him for really trying to understand the Christian point of view. In his book *A Faith for All Seasons* he writes, "it is indeed difficult to avoid being impressed by the peculiar content and sheer incredibleness of some Christian creedal claims. It may fairly be said, at the risk of sounding polemical and unsympathetic, that among monotheistic creeds, embrace of Christianity requires assent to the largest collection of highly implausible beliefs."[1] He goes on to write, "Complexity . . . is one thing, incoherence another. Paradox is one thing, nonsense another."[2] The Christian faith involves itself in nonsense, he believes, by claiming that God is one in three and three in one—that's the basic charge that we hear from the Muslim point of view.

Sproul: As you indicated earlier, it is not just this particular scholar who lays the charge of incoherent nonsense at our feet with respect to the Trinity; many others, such as Thomas Jefferson and Immanuel Kant, have complained about its incomprehensibility. Abraham Lincoln struggled virtually his

whole life with the idea. And one of the things that I appreci-
ate about Shabbir Akhtar is that he was able to make a distinction between paradox and nonsense, and between
incoherence and complexity. He also raised the question of
incomprehensibility.

First of all, Islam is not the only religion that is passionately
committed to monotheism. Historic Judaism is as well. And no
religion is more passionately committed to monotheism than
Christianity. Christianity understands its doctrine of the Trinity
as affirming monotheism. The very word *trinity* is a combina-
tion of "tri" and "unity," and the accent is on the unity; trinity
is not tri-theism. Always and everywhere, Christianity has resis-
ted any heretical idea that there are three parts to God, that
there are three beings or three gods in any polytheistic way.

As the Islamic scholar said, "Complexity is one thing, incoherence another." I am amazed at how often the doctrine of the
Trinity is charged with being irrational and contradictory.
Jefferson, in his complaint, talked about the irrational arithmetic—three in one and one in three. We need to go back to
the elementary principles of rationality and learn—or review—
the distinctions among these three categories: contradiction,
paradox, and mystery.

The classical definition of contradiction, by the philosopher Aristotle in his system of logic—which he called the
"organon" of all science, the necessary instrument for all mean-
ingful discourse—was this: something cannot be what it is
and *not* be what it is at the same time and in the same relationship. The shorthand for that is, "A cannot be A and non-
A at the same time and in the same relationship." For example,

I can be a father (A) and a son (B) at the same time, but not in the same relationship. The doctrine of the Trinity is often called a contradiction; I'm going to try to show that it is not. But first, let's understand what a contradiction is. If I say that something is what it is and is not what it is at the same time and in the same relationship, I would be guilty of violating the law of non-contradiction.

A paradox, on the other hand, is not a contradiction. The "dox" in paradox comes from the Greek *dokeo,* which means "to seem, to think, or to appear." "Docetism" comes from the same root. The heretical Docetists denied that Jesus had a true body. They said that He was a phantom; He only seemed to be human. *Para* means "alongside"; thus *paradox* means that something seems like something else when placed alongside it. A paradox is not a contradiction. It is an *apparent* contradiction; when you look at it more closely and give it the benefit of the second glance, you can see that, in fact, the terms are not really contradictory.

A paradox may be jarring to the ear. Paul said that I have to become a slave in order to be free (Rom. 6:15-23). That sounds contradictory, but when we examine it, we see that he means I have to be a slave in one sense in order to be free in another sense. Otherwise, he would be talking nonsense. He is using paradox, a perfectly legitimate literary form that is used frequently in many religions and elsewhere.

The third category, mystery, is the one that most often is confused with contradiction. In many courses on Christian theology the first lecture is on the incomprehensibility of God. This does not mean that God is completely unknowable, but rather that no human has an exhaustive, categorical understanding of the mind of God; we cannot know God in His exhaustive fullness. Muhammad would agree with that: God has revealed Himself to a degree that we can understand, but there are also dimensions of God that are beyond our human understanding. God is infinite in His perspective, but we can never have an infinite perspective of anything because we are finite. An infinite perspective is beyond our ability. This is axiomatic in Islamic theology, in Jewish theology, and in Christian theology.

We all agree that there are incomprehensible elements to truth. This is also true in the secular, scientific community. There are many phenomena, such as gravity and motion, that we would affirm are real but that we do not yet completely understand. However, it is one thing to say that something is mysterious, that we do not understand it; it is quite another thing to say that it is contradictory or nonsensical or absurd.

Here is where the confusion comes. I don't understand mysteries; that's why we call them mysteries. I also don't understand contradictions. If you said to me, "There is no God, and Mary is His mother," I would not understand what you were saying. I had a theology professor who once said, "God is absolutely immutable in His being, and God is absolutely mutable in His being." The students said, "Wow! This guy's really deep." I thought, "This guy is really confused, because he just gave us a clear contradiction." Nobody could understand it, and they thought that he had given us a mystery. But what he had actually given us was a contradiction; the reason we couldn't understand it was that it was inherently non-understandable. Neither mysteries nor contradictions can be understood, but the difference is this: A mystery is not inherently unintelligible; it does not violate the law of non-contradiction. A contradiction does violate this law.

Can I penetrate the essence of the Trinity? No. There are mysterious, incomprehensible elements to it. However, there is nothing contradictory about it.

The church historically has been very careful in setting forth this definition of the Trinity: God is one in essence, three in person. God is one single being but three persons. He is one in A, but three in B. The plurality is in a different category from the category of being. The church speaks of three "subsistences" within God, not three distinct essences.

No one can demonstrate that the formula for the Trinity breaks the law of non-contradiction. If the trinitarian formula violated the law of non-contradiction, I would reject it in a heartbeat. But the truth is that the doctrine of the Trinity is neither irrational nor nonsensical nor contradictory.

The church historically has made it very clear that the distinctions in the Godhead are *not essential,* in the sense that they are not referring to three distinct essences or beings. God is only one being or essence. We are monotheists with respect to the essential being of God Himself. But at the same time, we are saying, within the being of God, underneath it, subsisting within that one being, are three distinct personae. However, these personae do not differ from each other in essence, so it is not a distinction in their essence. We distinguish within God, even as the Muslims and the Jews do, the various attributes of God—that God is eternal and God is immutable.

That does not mean that there are two different parts of God, that one part is immutable and one part is eternal. Rather, God is immutably eternal and eternally immutable. If we do not carve up God into various aspects, we're not damaging His essence when we distinguish among His attributes. The church affirms this same principle with respect to the Trinity.

The doctrine of the Trinity is based on the New Testament teaching on the nature of Christ. The church affirms the Trinity because the New Testament distinguishes between God and His eternal Logos, or the Word.

Saleeb: Could you say something about how belief in the Trinity is relevant to the Christian believer?

Sproul: Let me pose a question: If Christ is God incarnate, what significance does that have for my life when He gives commands? It is one thing to receive moral suggestions from a great teacher. It is another thing altogether to have commands imposed upon me by God incarnate. This makes all the difference in the world with respect to my practice. That is a very practical consequence of the doctrine of the Trinity. If I believe in the Trinity—if I believe that Jesus is a member of the triune Godhead—I cannot dismiss Him as merely an insightful moral teacher.

One thing that bothers me about Islam and Judaism is that, though they deny the deity of Christ, they exalt Him as a prophet. If they were consistent, they would say that this man is a false prophet because the very center core of Christ's prophetic teaching was about Himself: His identity, His relationship to the Father, and the authority that He carries. We need to emphasize that Jesus did, in fact, claim to be more than a prophet, and more than just an insightful teacher of wisdom.

The ministry of the Holy Spirit is also an integral part of the Christian life and another manifestation of the Trinity. The Holy Spirit is God working in us and for us, helping us in our quest for sanctification. I don't know anything more practical than to know that my quest for obedience is not wrought simply in my own power, but that I have been empowered by God Himself to help accomplish the call that He has given to us. All Christians who live out the Christian life are intimately familiar with the practical implications of the ministry of the Spirit in their lives.

Saleeb: In *Mere Christianity*, C. S. Lewis writes that even in the simple act of prayer, when you as a believer kneel down by your bed and pray to the Father, in the name of the Son, through the Spirit, you are involved in the life of the Trinity. You are talking to God, but it is God in you who is drawing you to Himself, and this relationship has been established because of Jesus Christ.[3]

So the doctrine of the Trinity is not just a doctrine we pay lip service to: it has ramifications for every aspect of our Christian life and worship.

4

ISLAM AND CHRISTIANITY
ON SIN

Saleeb: I'd like to begin our discussion of the doctrine of man by briefly discussing the Islamic idea of what Christianity calls "salvation history." According to the Qur'an, there is a master-servant relationship between God and man. God created Adam and Eve, and they sinned. They repented. God forgave them. Basically, the whole history of salvation according to the Qur'an is that God has sent prophets throughout history to all people groups to guide them to the straight path—the straight path of worshiping one God, doing good deeds, looking forward to the day of judgment, and living in light of the day of judgment. This summarizes the Islamic understanding of God and His relationship to humanity.

The Qur'an contains several accounts of the creation story, which, on the surface, seem similar to the biblical account in Genesis. In Sura 2 God creates Adam and Eve. Sura 2:35-37 contains this account: "We said, 'Oh Adam! dwell thou and thy wife in the Garden; and eat of the bountiful things therein as (where and when) ye will; but approach not this tree, or ye run into harm and transgression.' Then did Satan make them slip from the (Garden), and get them out of the state (of felicity) in which they had been. We said: 'Get ye down all (ye people), with enmity between yourselves. On earth will be your dwelling place.' . . . Then learnt Adam from his Lord words of inspiration, and his Lord turned towards him; for He is oft-returning, Most Merciful."

According to this account, Adam and Eve were created in a state of righteousness in paradise. They disobeyed God's command to not eat of the forbidden tree, and they were expelled from paradise to earth (this differs, of course, from the biblical account). But when they were expelled, God forgave them. Adam, in fact, became the first prophet. And, according to Islamic theology, prophets are kept from fundamental, or major, sins, because they must be more pure than the rest of us to be the means of receiving God's revelation. The Qur'anic story, on the surface, might seem similar to the biblical account: that Adam was created righteous, and then he sinned and fell. But Islamic theology actually has no room for any doctrine of the fall of man. Adam sinned. God forgave him. That's the end of the story. Adam's sin had no consequence for people who came after Adam.

Shabbir Akhtar writes, "Islam . . . sees the Fall as simply one powerful and contained manifestation of evil—more accurately, disobedience to God's will—that has no larger implications for human nature in general or even for Adam's nature in particular. Adam ate the forbidden fruit; Allah forgave him, for Allah does what he pleases. Indeed, Muslims view Adam's expulsion from Eden as the occasion for the 'Rise' of man. Adam's original disobedience to God's will is seen as being merely the joint result of ignorance and *akrasia* (weakness of will). Therefore, men need only mentors and the grace of God."[1] Islam believes that humankind is not sinful by nature.

The Qur'an does use such terms as "ignorant," "weak-willed," "arrogant," "easily led astray," and "ungrateful" to describe human nature. However, man is not seen as essentially fallen or sinful. Isma'il al-Faruqi, a prominent Muslim theologian, writes, "Islam teaches that people are born innocent and remain so until each makes him or herself guilty by a guilty deed. Islam does not believe in 'original sin'; and its scripture interprets Adam's disobedience as his own personal misdeed— a misdeed for which he repented and which God forgave."[2] For Muslims that's the end of the story. In this understanding, we have no bad news to tell Muslims—that they are sinners and need salvation; therefore, there is no room for telling them good news later on. This is, of course, another fundamental difference between Islam and Christianity.

Regarding the doctrine of man, Islam finds itself much in agreement with many people in the Western world today. Ads for the U.S. Army used the slogan, "Be all that you can be." Muslims say that Christianity makes man a weak creature who is fallen and in desperate need of help, but Islam gives him dignity. It says, "Rise up! You are morally capable of fulfilling God's will for yourself! You can do it! You can take actions for yourself and your neighborhood and clean up your society." That is another significant point of difference between the Christian and Islamic understandings of humankind.

Sproul: You said earlier that contemporary Muslim critics of Christianity maintain that they have great allies in their debates from not only Enlightenment thinkers and Western philosophers but also Christian theologians who support their contentions. You also mentioned a poll indicating that a majority of evangelical Christians believe that humankind is basically good. In the history of Christianity there are basically only three subdivisions of theology: the Pelagian school, the Semi-Pelagian school, and the Augustinian school. When we say that some Christian teachers or theologians promote views similar to those of Muslim critics, criticizing orthodox Christianity, one of the problems that arises is the question of who is a Christian. Several years ago, when I looked up the word *Christian* in the dictionary, there were several definitions. The last one defined a Christian as "one who is civilized." In other words, anybody who is civilized could be called a Christian. But when I use the term *Christian,* I'm referring to classic, orthodox, historic Christianity. Throughout the history of the church, it has had to deal with heretics and with heretical movements that were deemed so antithetical to historic and biblical Christianity that people were excommunicated or dismissed from fellowship within the church.

For centuries, advocates of Semi-Pelagianism and of Augustinianism have struggled with each other theologically. Within historical Christianity that struggle, for the most part, has been viewed as an intramural debate among Christians. Both Semi-Pelagianism and Augustinianism believe in original sin; the debate is over the extent of the original sin. But Pelagianism, which was condemned as heretical early on in church history, denies original sin. Pelagians take the position that Adam's sin affected Adam and only Adam, that sin did not have the power to distort, in any way, the nature of humankind. That is basically the Muslim view as well.

Thus, before Muhammad, there was Pelagius, teaching this same idea and objecting to the doctrine of original sin. That doctrine, taught by Pelagius, that was deemed sub-Christian and even anti-Christian in the fourth and fifth centuries, was resurrected in the sixteenth century in the Socinian heresy, which also denied original sin. It was resurrected again in the nineteenth century, with nineteenth-century liberalism on the one hand, and on the other hand with Charles Finney, who claimed to be an evangelical yet denied any transfer of guilt from Adam to his descendants.

There are also many today within the neo-liberal and radical left schools who profess to be Christian yet who deny the fall of man and original sin. However, when we examine all of the historic creeds of all of the various denominations—Lutheran, Episcopalian, Methodist, Roman Catholic, and so on, we see that every one of them has some doctrine of original sin. This is because the Bible makes it so clear that what happened to Adam had radical consequences for the whole human race—that the whole human race fell together with Adam, and that we are born in a state of corruption. This is underscored by the teaching of Jesus Himself.

Jonathan Edwards, the great Puritan theologian, wrote one of the most important and definitive monographs on original sin. After examining the biblical teaching on original sin, he turned his attention to what he called natural reason. He argued that even if the Bible didn't teach a doctrine of original sin, natural reason would require it in order to explain the universality of human corruption. If all people are born innocent, if all people are born without any bent or inclination toward sin or wickedness, why then do we have the almost universal recognition that nobody is perfect, that everybody sins?

Even humanists will admit that we are not perfect. They claim that we are basically good, that at the core of our being is goodness. But they'll admit that sin is there, on the periphery, as it were. The evangelical Christians in the poll we discussed earlier who believe that man is basically good would also acknowledge that we're all sinners. They simply fail to see how deep that sin goes.

Edwards argued, if it is the case that we are all born innocent, it would seem that at least fifty percent of the people would stay that way. Why is it that we have a hundred percent of the people slipping into some kind of corruption? According to Edwards, the universality of this corruption is evidence that there is something wrong with the very moral nature of human beings. Some, including Muslims, respond to that by saying, "People are born innocent, as Rousseau said, and it is society that corrupts them."

This response begs the question, How did society get corrupt in the first place? Societies are composed of individuals. And if mankind is basically good, one would assume that at least some societies would be *without* corruption.

The fundamental problem in wrestling with the sinful nature of man—in all of these schemas, whether secular humanism, Pelagianism, or the Islamic view—is a radical difference in our understanding of God. In the final analysis, our understanding of God determines our evaluation of the righteousness of man. Any time the holiness of God is in any way diminished, the standard for righteousness and holiness is diminished with it. Once that standard is lowered, we can flatter ourselves regarding our own performance as human beings and, as Calvin once said, address ourselves as something only a little less than demigods.

However, we must examine ourselves in light of the ultimate standard of righteousness, which is God's character as presented in the Bible. God, who created humankind, calls us to be perfect and holy even as He is holy (1 Pet. 1:16). Thus, the standard by which good and evil are to be measured is God's character itself.

Paul, writing to the Corinthians, makes this observation: "But they, measuring themselves by themselves, and comparing themselves among themselves, are not wise" (2 Cor. 10:12). If I compare myself with other people, as long as I can find someone whose wickedness seems to be more heinous and egregious than my own, I can easily flatter myself into thinking that somehow I have arrived at an acceptable state of righteousness in the sight of God.

However, the minute we lift our gaze to God Himself and examine ourselves from the vertical standard of *His* righteousness, we suddenly see our own sinfulness. This is what happened to Isaiah when he saw a glimpse of the holiness of God and was undone (Isaiah 6); to Habakkuk when he trembled before the manifestation of the holiness of God (Hab. 3:16); to Job (Job 42:1-6); and to the disciples when they realized the full purity of the Christ with whom they were dealing (e.g., Luke 5:8; John 6:69). All of a sudden, by contrast, they saw their sinfulness.

When we fail to do this, we can falsely conclude that we live in a safe haven of righteousness where there really isn't any need for salvation—no need for an atonement. There's no need for redemption because there's nothing to be redeemed from.

Saleeb: In the Qur'an, God is portrayed in highly majestic and sovereign terms; however, in the entire Qur'an, the word *holy* is attributed to God only twice. In one verse in Isaiah, "Holy, holy, holy" (Isa. 6:3), there are more references to the holiness of God than in the entire Islamic scripture. This has shaped the limited Muslim understanding of the holiness of God. Further, orthodox Muslims do not believe that God has revealed His character or His righteousness. They say that God has revealed His will and His commands. However, that will and those commands do not reflect God's righteous and holy character, because we cannot know God. His law is not based on His own character.

Because of that understanding of God, and the diminished view of how holy He is, it is obviously very hard for Muslims to understand how sinful we are, and the radical nature of human sinfulness.

Sproul: In the final analysis, all of the issues of theology, sooner or later, come back to the primary issue: how we understand the nature and character of God. Some news commentators say, "We all believe in the same God." Larry King had a Muslim, a

Jewish rabbi, some Roman Catholics, and some Protestants on his program. He asked a Protestant on the program, "Do you believe that God is a Christian?" He responded, "No, He's the God of everybody." Well, that's true: the God we believe in is the God of everybody; there's only one true God. However, his answer ducked the question. Christianity's understanding of God is radically different from Islam's. We have to cut through the fog because the media blare this message every day: "Everybody believes in the same God; we just go to Him by different paths." This is simply not true.

Saleeb: How do you respond to someone who asks, "Is it fair that we are born with this sinful nature?"

Sproul: On the surface, it doesn't seem fair, and that is why the church has struggled with the concept of original sin. The Bible says that we fell in Adam (Rom. 5:12; 1 Cor. 15:22). Different theories have attempted to explain this; the basic point is that when Adam sinned, his action affected not only himself but all those whom he represented, the entire human race. It is a complicated matter, but the New Testament certainly makes it clear that there is a link between the sin of Adam and the sins of all mankind, and this is found in the Old Testament as well. Even David said, "I was brought forth in iniquity, and in sin my mother conceived me" (Ps. 51:5), acknowledging that he was corrupt from birth.

ISLAM AND CHRISTIANITY ON SALVATION

Saleeb: The Islamic view of salvation differs radically from the Christian view. As we discussed earlier, Islam and Christianity disagree on the doctrine of sin. Most Muslims do not view sin as radically as Christians do; they view sin as simply actions. When we witness to Muslims, it is crucial that we share with them passages like the Sermon on the Mount to show that the biblical view of sin takes us much deeper into heart issues than just superficial actions.

Since Islam does not view sin as a radical problem, it is very natural that salvation, for Islam, also is not as radical a solution as the Christian faith claims. Basically, Islam claims that salvation is earned by good works. There are many passages in the Qur'an about the day of judgment, about the punishment of hell and the rewards of paradise. One of the images in the Qur'an is that of a scale. On the day of judgment, all your works will be weighed: "Then those whose balance (of good deeds) is heavy—they will attain salvation: but those whose balance is light, will be those who have lost their souls; in hell will they abide" (Sura 23:102-103). Faith is important, but works are essential for salvation. There is hope of salvation, but no assurance.

I referred earlier to Isma'il al-Faruqi, a Muslim theologian. Here he compares Islam with Christianity:

> Assuming all men necessarily to be 'fallen', to stand in the predicament of 'original sin', of 'alienation from God', of self-contradiction, self-centeredness, or of 'falling short of the perfection of God', Christian mission seeks to ransom and save. Islam holds man to be not in need of any salvation. Instead of assuming him to be religiously and ethically fallen, Islamic *da'wah* acclaims him as the *khalifah* of Allah, perfect in form, and endowed with all that is necessary to fulfill the divine will indeed, even loaded with the grace of revelation. . . . 'Salvation' is hence not in the vocabulary of Islam. . . . Islam understands itself as man's assumption of his cosmic role as the one for whose sake creation was created. He is its innocent, perfect and moral master; and every part of it is his to have and to enjoy. He is called to obey, i.e. to fulfill the will of Allah. But this fulfillment is in and of space and time.[1]

Basically al-Faruqi is saying that man, " . . . as Islam defines him, is not an object of salvation, but its subject."[2]

Muslims generally have a confident view that humankind is basically good. God has given man the moral ability to perform deeds of righteousness, to obey God; by obeying God and fulfilling His commands, man can have *hope* of salvation. However, there is no *assurance* of salvation. Earlier I referred to a recent study done by Fuller Seminary based on interviews of six hundred former Muslims who have come to Jesus Christ. The number one factor in their conversion, in the vast majority of these people, was the issue of the Christian assurance of salvation. Islam is very dogmatic that not just faith alone but works of righteousness and believing and obeying the commands of God, as defined in the Qur'an, are the means to salvation; in that sense it is very different from the Christian position.

Many years ago a group of Christians visited the imam (spiritual leader) of a mosque in Chicago. An African-American, he had converted from Christianity to Islam. They asked him why he had left Christianity and had become a Muslim. He answered, "Islam offers a way for emasculated men to become something. Christianity, on the other hand, is a welfare religion—'Jesus paid it all'—and my people don't need that." According to him, Christianity turns men into weak creatures who are helpless and hopeless and need a savior. Islam gives dignity to men. It says, "You can do it. You can stand on your feet. God has given you these abilities; get up and take responsibility for your own destiny and your own soul." This is basically the Islamic view of salvation.

Sproul: The imam's comments are reminiscent of Friedrich Nietzsche, who complained that the soft underbelly of western Europe was the direct result of the "weakness religion" propagated by Christianity, which elevated virtues of mercy and grace rather than strength and courage, thus undermining the strength of the existential hero. We find this perspective also in

modern existential heroes like Sartre and Camus, and even in
the popular writings of Ernest Hemingway and others who
complain that Christianity is for the weak and for those who
have lost their humanity and have been emasculated.

Abdul, you have read statements from the Qur'an about salvation, at least with respect to a different destiny—some going
to paradise, some going to hell. Then you read from one of the
Muslim theologians, who said that salvation is not part of their
vocabulary. What exactly is salvation to a Muslim? Salvation
from what? Does salvation mean being rescued from hell?

Saleeb: Yes, that is what Islam believes. The Muslim theologians I quoted are exaggerating their claim, to contrast Islam
with Christianity. Muslims do believe strongly that there is a
heaven and a hell, and that they need to live in light of that fact.
However, the word *salvation* does not appear much in the
Qur'an. Thus, Islamic and Christian terminologies are different, as are the means of attaining salvation.

Sproul: In Islam as in Christianity, it is God who determines
each person's destiny—hell or paradise—and He does it on
some basis. In Islam, the basis is a weighing on the scale of
justice: if a person's good deeds outweigh his bad deeds, then he
goes to paradise. And if the scale is unbalanced in the other
direction, he goes to hell. This assumes some standard that God
uses to discern whether they're going to the one place or the
other, and all that is required to satisfy the justice of God is
that the scales not be weighted more in the direction of sin than
in the direction of virtue.

However, if someone's good outweighs his evil, God, who is supposedly a just judge, does not seem to sense any obligation to punish the evil. In that case God simply forgives the evil. In this scheme God seems to be somewhat arbitrary, not entirely just.

It all comes back to our understanding of the character of God. If God is holy, and He measures my sin against His holiness, it would be impossible to even balance the scales. David said, "If You, LORD, should mark iniquities, O Lord, who could stand?" (Ps. 130:3). The question raised by historical Judaism is, What human being could possibly survive the perfect judgment of a perfect God? If God is perfectly just, how can I—as an unjust person, with my iniquities—stand that judgment? The Muslim answer is, You can stand it very well as long as you balance the scale.

Recall Belshazzar's feast and the words on the wall: *Mene, mene, tekel, upharsin,* that is, "You have been weighed in the balances, and found wanting" (Dan. 5:27). And God's judgment falls on Belshazzar. Recall Amos talking about the measuring rod by which God measures people, and He finds that they are all falling short of His standard (Amos 7:7-9). This is also the message of the New Testament: God is so righteous and so holy that He requires from us perfection, so that if we sin just one time—and we sin far more than that—we become indebted to Him in terms of His justice. We are now sinners who cannot pay our debt. This is the way the Bible describes the human predicament: we are debtors who do not have the capacity to pay our debt.

A Muslim would say, "I may be a debtor, but I can pay

the debt by making up for my deficit with meritorious works that outweigh my demerits." That would work in a schema where God did not require perfection; but if He requires perfection, and I sin once, what can I possibly do to make up for my deficit? If I do everything perfectly the rest of my life, I am simply doing what I'm required to do in the first place. I become, in the words of Jesus, merely an "unprofitable servant" (Luke 17:10).

Saleeb: One Muslim author, in dialogue with a Christian author, writes this: "Islam does not identify with the Christian conviction that man needs to be redeemed. The Christian belief in the redemptive sacrificial death of Christ does not fit the Islamic view that man has always been fundamentally good, and that God loves and forgives those who obey His will."[3] So basically it comes back to our understanding of how sinful we are and how holy God is. The Qur'an does have many passages about how ungrateful human beings are, how easily they are led astray, how much they transgress and disobey God, but Islamic theology hasn't paid much attention to that aspect of the Qur'an.

Sproul: This issue is very much alive within the Christian community. It is difficult to find Christians who have a strong sense of the seriousness of sin. A majority of professing Christians are still resting upon the confidence they have in their own works to get them into heaven.

However, this is not the biblical view; it is a humanist view that has invaded the Christian community. Some contemporary manifestations of Christianity are hardly different from some aspects of Islam. That's why I keep speaking in terms of historic, orthodox, biblical Christianity. We need to make that distinction from many of the contemporary versions of Christianity, which for the most part have repudiated the essential teachings of Christ and of the New Testament.

Saleeb: Something that helped me profoundly in my growth in understanding the nature of sin was your discussion in *The Holiness of God*[4] on Martin Luther's struggle with how sinful we are. We must communicate to Muslims that by *sin* we do not just mean stealing and adultery and murder and all the big items; sin is a much deeper issue in our hearts. Could you expound on that?

Sproul: Luther, being trained in law, would look at the law of God, first of all in the Old Testament. He would ask questions such as, What is the great commandment? Well, the great commandment is, "You shall love the LORD your God with all your heart, with all your soul and with all your mind. . . . [and] You shall love your neighbor as yourself" (Matt. 22:37, 39). And Luther would scratch his head and say, "Let me see if I understand this. The great commandment is that God requires me to love Him with all of my heart—all of my heart, not some of my heart. My affection has to be total and complete."

And then he would turn his gaze inward to examine his own soul and say, "I haven't loved God with all of my heart for five minutes in my lifetime, but what about with all of my mind? I've been a student; I've studied the Bible and theology.

I've been somewhat disciplined in my pursuit of truth. But at the same time, I haven't loved God with all of my mind. I haven't applied myself absolutely perfectly with every ounce of energy in the pursuit of the truth of God. I certainly haven't used all of my strength in loving Him, and that's only half of the great commandment. I'm also supposed to love my neighbor as much as myself, and the Bible defines the neighbor as everybody out there. How can I love everybody in the world as much as I love myself? I'm in trouble!"

Luther would then say, "If that's the great commandment, then the violation of that commandment would have to be the great transgression." At that point Luther differs from most human beings, who would say, "Nobody loves God with all his heart and all his soul and all his mind, and nobody in the world loves everybody else in the world as much as he loves himself. Nobody does that, so it can't be that important."

We continue to reduce the standard to the level that we can achieve, and that's where we deceive ourselves. One of the hardest things in the world in the church today is to get people concerned about the gospel. The reason is that we have so obscured the law of God that the gospel isn't even good news anymore because there's no *bad* news with which to contrast it. Many nominal Christians assume the grace of God; they presume that they're going to heaven. In this respect, there's no real difference between the Muslim and the nominal Christian. They assume that they're good enough to get past the bar of God's righteousness.

In my book on the holiness of God I put a searchlight on Isaiah's response to God's holiness. Before he got a glimpse of the holiness of God, Isaiah was considered the most righteous man in the nation, but when he saw who God was, he disintegrated. He fell apart and pronounced a curse upon himself, because for the first time in his life he understood who he was against the backdrop of the character of God. As long as we can keep the character of God in eclipse and can conceal from our vision who He is, we can continue to flatter ourselves that we can balance the scales of justice or earn our way into the kingdom of God. This is the greatest human delusion there is.

Saleeb: The issue of assurance of salvation is also very relevant. Islam is very emphatic that nobody will know his destiny until the day of judgment. As al-Faruqi explains, the scale of justice "is infinite, and there is no point at which Muslims may carry their titles to paradise, as it were, in their pockets. Everyone strives, and some strive more than others. . . . Religious justification is thus the Muslims' eternal hope, never their complacent certainty, nor for even a fleeting moment."[5] Because of this, many Muslims die in fear because they don't know. Many suspect that the balance of their scale is probably not going to be tipped in the right direction.

But what is the Christian view of assurance of salvation? Do we need to be afraid in our life that at the moment of death we might not be aware of our eternal destiny?

Sproul: We do not need to be afraid; in fact, we're commanded to make our salvation and election sure (2 Pet. 1:10). According to the promises of God in the New Testament, there is a basis for having an assurance of salvation; that assurance rests not upon my own righteousness but upon God's promise to redeem all of those who put their trust in Christ and in Christ alone. If we indeed abandon all hope of redeeming ourselves and instead place our trust in Christ, that trust gives us the assurance that Christ is able to redeem us and that God, who is a God of truth, will keep His promise. Hence, our assurance is based upon the surety of His word and of His work on our behalf.

If we simply trust in doing our best, our best will only get us into hell; our best is simply not good enough. My assurance is based on *Christ's* best, on what He has done for us. That's why this quest for salvation, in the final analysis, is directly related to the atonement. One of the big differences between Christianity and other religions is that they don't have an atonement. They claim that they don't need it.

My response is, what you don't have is the thing you need more desperately than anything else, unless you want to actually stand on the basis of your own righteousness before a just and holy God. If you think you can survive that judgment, you are tragically mistaken.

ISLAM AND CHRISTIANITY ON THE DEATH OF CHRIST

Saleeb: Muslims deny both Jesus' death on the cross and His deity. Yet they do genuinely believe in Jesus and honor Him as a great prophet. The Qur'an mentions Jesus dozens of times and gives Jesus many honorary titles, for example, the "Messiah" or "Christ" (e.g., 4:157), the "word from God" (e.g., 3:45), a "spirit" from God (e.g., 4:171), and a "sign" (e.g., 23:50). The Qur'an also claims that Jesus was born of the virgin Mary. And the Qur'an claims that Jesus did many miracles, including raising people from the dead. Further, the Qur'an claims that Jesus is alive today, and, according to Sunni Muslims, He will return before the resurrection of humankind to set the world straight.

Muslims assume that they already believe everything that needs to be believed about Jesus, and that they already honor Him as one of the greatest prophets, maybe second only to Muhammad. Many of them are genuinely shocked when a Christian approaches them and says, "You need to trust in

Jesus." They respond, "We do. We already believe in Jesus, and our holy book says many beautiful things about Jesus and what He said and what He did." And in fact, in the Islamic cultures around the world, Jesus has a very special place in the hearts of many people.

In the Qur'an we read: "That they [the Jews] said (in boast), 'We killed Christ Jesus, the Son of Mary, the Messenger of Allah'—but they killed him not, nor crucified him, but so it was made to appear to them, and those who differ therein are full of doubts, with no (certain) knowledge, but only conjecture to follow, for of a surety they killed him not—nay, Allah raised him up unto Himself; and Allah is exalted in Power, Wise . . ." (Sura 4:157-158). Many Muslim commentators throughout history have proposed various hypotheses about the meaning of this passage. Maybe Judas was mistakenly crucified instead of Jesus. Perhaps God put the likeness of Jesus on somebody else. One of the disciples might have volunteered to die in the place of the master. But whatever happened, the Qur'an makes it very clear that Jesus never died on the cross. However, it was made to appear to people as if Jesus had been crucified. Thus, God was involved in some kind of deceit to save the great honored prophet Jesus.

Kenneth Cragg, a Christian scholar of Islam, has explained what he calls Islam's three denials with regard to the cross. There is the "historical denial of its actuality." This is what we just read in the Qur'an—the claim that the cross never actually happened. There is "the moral refusal of its possibility." Muslims believe that prophets of God cannot be so humiliated or die such shameful deaths; God would never allow His honored prophets to end like that. He has always rescued His prophets from danger. And there is the "doctrinal rejection of its necessity."[1] Since we do not need to be saved from our sinfulness, we don't need someone to die for us; we are all responsible for our own moral actions and for our own salvation. Hence, there is no need for a cross or an atonement. This is a huge point of contrast between Islam and Christianity.

The source that Muslims appeal to for their understanding and information about Christ is not the New Testament but the Qur'an. They say that this book was revealed to Muhammad six hundred years after Christ, and they accept whatever this book says about Him. When the Qur'an gives titles to Jesus—such as the Messiah, the spirit of God, the word of God—it has no understanding of what these titles signify; for example, it has no understanding of what the Messiah was supposed to be according to the Old Testament.

It is especially difficult to witness to Muslims because, on the one hand, they concede so much about Jesus, but on the other hand, they take away the most foundational truths about the Christian faith. It is also difficult for Muslims to make sense of why somebody had to die on a cross for our sins two thousand years ago.

Sproul: When Muslims claim that Jesus didn't actually die, I believe that what they're really saying is that they don't like the Christian understanding of the meaning and significance of that death.

This goes back to the questions of salvation and of the justice of God. The issue in the New Testament is this: when I sin against God, I incur a debt. I have an obligation to obey Him, and when I disobey Him, I am now morally indebted to Him. Also, I have committed a crime against His law, and I have violated our personal relationship.

Thus, we have a debt, a violation of the relationship, and a crime. All three of these are involved every time I sin against God. The Bible describes our sins as debts that we are incapable of paying for ourselves. If somebody came to me today and said, "We've noticed here in our books that you owe us $10,000," that would be difficult for me to pay, but I could do it. If someone said, "You owe $10 billion, and you have three days to pay," it is within the realm of possibility that I could come up with $10 billion to pay my debt in the next three days. Maybe I could find somebody who has $100 billion who would take mercy on me and give me the $10 billion to pay my debt. But, of course, the odds are astronomical against that happening.

However, my debt before God is not $10 billion. It is a moral debt that is infinite, and I have no capacity whatever to pay the debt. Only someone with a superficial notion of sin can talk about man's ability to make up for his own sins by himself. But I understand that my transgressions against God put me absolutely in debt to Him, that I've committed a crime against Him, that I've violated my relationship to Him, and finally that I am not capable of satisfying His justice, of meeting my obligations. If I want salvation in terms of rescue from God's judgment and rescue from the destiny of hell, then what I desperately need is a savior, someone who will pay the debt for me.

This story will illustrate the difference between a pecuniary debt and a moral debt. A little boy goes into the ice cream shop and orders a two-scoop ice cream cone. The proprietor behind the counter hands him the two-scoop cone and says, "That will be two dollars." The boy becomes crestfallen. He reaches into his pocket, pulls out a dollar bill and says, "But my mommy only gave me one dollar." If I'm there watching, I will reach into my pocket, take out a dollar, hand it to the owner, and tell her, "Here's the other dollar. Let the boy have his cone." This illustrates a pecuniary debt. The boy owed that woman a dollar, and I paid it with legal tender. She has to accept that payment and give the boy his cone.

Let's change the scenario a little bit. The boy asks for the cone, and the woman hands it to him. He turns around and runs out the door without paying. She yells, "Stop! Thief!" A policeman walking down the street grabs the boy by the scruff of his neck, brings him back into the store, and asks, "What's going on here?" The woman replies, "He just stole that ice cream cone. It's worth two dollars." I step forward and say, "Wait a minute, officer. Let him go. I'll pay the two dollars." In this case, does the owner have to accept that payment? No. Can the owner accept the payment and not press charges? Yes, but it is up to the owner, the one who has been violated, the one to whom the debt is owed, as to whether she will receive payment for the ice cream by another agent.

That is the glory of the gospel: God accepts payment for sin by a substitute, who willingly pays my debt. Because in accepting that payment, God manifests His grace and His mercy, and at the same time the debt is paid. God is not only merciful; He is also just. He also sees that sin is punished.

There's actually a two-way transfer here. Our redemption is not just by the cross; it is also by the life of Jesus. My guilt is transferred to Jesus, and His righteousness is transferred to me by God, through imputation. Muslims may not agree with that, but God certainly has the right to redeem man on that basis if He so desires. This is what the gospel of New Testament Christianity proclaims: that this is exactly what took place in the person and work of Jesus Christ. Christ stood in our stead, stepped into the gap where we were incapable of satisfying the commands and demands of God, and did that work for us. My message to the Muslim is, "You have two options: You can face the judgment of God on the basis of your own righteousness, or you can face it on the basis of somebody else's righteousness." I would much rather stand before God on the basis of Christ's righteousness than on the basis of my own righteousness.

Saleeb: Muslims claim that this theology of atonement is pagan thinking that has invaded Christianity and corrupted it. But the Christian message on atonement is basically a continuation of the themes found in the Old Testament. The heart of the Old Testament is the Torah, and the heart of the Torah is the book of Leviticus. In that book God institutes sacrifices for sin. Thus, substitutionary atonement finds its root in the Jewish Scriptures, and is continued in the New Testament. It is actually *Islam* that has deviated from this theology. The function of prophets was not simply to say, "Be ethical and do good." From the beginning God has said, "Sacrifices have to be made for atonement of our sins." We must emphasize to Muslims that the holiness of God and God's demand for substitutionary atonement have deep, biblical roots, not just from New Testament times but all the way back to the Old Testament.

ISLAM AND CHRISTIANITY ON
THE DEITY OF CHRIST

Saleeb: Islam rejects not only the death of Christ on the cross and the doctrine of the atonement, but also the deity of Christ. Jesus Christ is at the dividing point between Christianity and Islam. Following are several passages from the Qur'an on Christ's deity: "They do blaspheme who say: 'Allah is Christ the son of Mary.' But said Christ: 'O children of Israel! Worship Allah, my Lord and your Lord.' Whoever joins other gods with Allah, Allah will forbid him the Garden, and the Fire will be his abode" (Sura 5:72). "Christ, the son of Mary, was no more than a Messenger; many were the Messengers that passed away before him. His mother was a woman of truth. They had both to eat their (daily) food. See how Allah doth make His signs clear to them; yet see in what ways they are deluded away from the Truth!" (Sura 5:75). ". . . the Christians call Christ the Son of God. That is a saying from their mouth; (in this) they but imitate what the Unbelievers of old used to say. Allah's curse be on them: how they are deluded away from the Truth" (Sura 9:30).

Let's compare Sura 9:30 with 1 John 5:11-12: "And this is the testimony: that God has given us eternal life, and this life is in His Son. He who has the Son has life; he who does not have the Son of God does not have life." The Christian faith claims that believing in Jesus as God incarnate is the key to gaining eternal life. Islam says that calling Jesus the Son of God puts you under the curse of God. In fact, according to the Qur'an, God will forgive any sin except this sin of *shirk*, of attributing a partner to God. Islam claims that Christians are guilty of committing that unpardonable sin: we have elevated a human prophet, Jesus of Nazareth, to the same level as God.

The issue of the deity of Christ is not simply a matter of relatively inconsequential differences of opinions. In fact, both Christianity and Islam claim that your eternal destiny depends on how you answer the question that Jesus Himself asked: "Who do you say that I am?" (Matt. 16:15). Muslims feel completely justified in rejecting the deity of Christ. The Qur'an has many beautiful passages that talk about who Jesus was and what He did, yet it denies the death of Christ and the deity of Christ. And now Islam can find many allies among Christian scholars who have come to the same conclusions.

What Did Jesus Really Say? is the title of a famous book on Islamic polemics by Misha'al ibn Abdullah.[1] (It is also the subtitle of the famous Jesus Seminar book, *The Five Gospels: What Did Jesus Really Say?*[2]) The author quotes from a 1984 British newspaper article entitled "Shock Survey of Anglican Bishops." The article reports that a survey of England's Anglican bishops revealed that half of them say Christians are not obliged to believe that Jesus Christ was God. Further, a high percentage of these bishops themselves deny the deity of Christ and do not think that Christians need to believe in His deity. Muslims are fond of quoting books like *The Myth of God Incarnate*,[3] written by Christian scholars who say that Jesus was just another prophet, a man with great God-consciousness, and that only later did Christians elevate Him to divine status.

Some Muslims even point to biblical verses to deny Christ's deity. They say, "When Jesus was asked about His return, He said, 'The day or the hour knows no man, not even the Son. Only the Father knows.' When someone addressed Jesus as, 'Good teacher,' Jesus Himself replied, 'Why do you call me good? Only God is good.' Your own Bible presents to us a Jesus who is a human being, who is just a prophet from God, and you Christians have committed the sin of elevating this human being to the divine. You need to repent of this and have the correct understanding of who Jesus really was."

Sproul: We hear all the time that both Christianity and Islam are true, but you have articulated well their radically different views of Christ. Even a cursory examination of these religions shows that they are radically incompatible, and nowhere is that more evident than with respect to their views on the person of Christ. Christianity is called *Christianity*, not "Godianity," because of the central role and importance of Jesus Christ. A radically different view of Him is what separates Christianity from other world religions—not only Islam, but all other religions.

You said that the Muslim critics of Christianity are fond of quoting our own Christian scholars who have questioned the deity of Christ. But how can we really even call these people Christians? Throughout its history, whenever the church has met in council over the deity of Christ, those who rejected the deity of Christ were considered heretical, not part of orthodox Christianity.

The church has indeed faced a crisis with respect to the person of Christ in every age, most strenuously in four centuries—the fourth, fifth, nineteenth, and twentieth centuries. The fourth-century controversy culminated in the Council of Nicea, which clearly affirmed the deity of Christ; the fifth century culminated in the Council of Chalcedon in 451, which again affirmed the deity of Christ. In nineteenth-century and twentieth-century liberalism and neo-liberalism, some people within the church, such as the Anglican bishops you mentioned, denied the deity of Christ. But when they did that, they were, in my judgment, consciously stepping outside orthodox, historic, biblical Christianity. What we are trying to focus on here is Islam vis-a-vis orthodox Christianity, not apostate Christianity.

Saleeb: Muslims do not make that distinction: they view them all as Christians.

Sproul: I agree that Muslims do have allies within the church. To address Jesus' limit of knowledge when He was asked about His return (Mark 13:32), we need to examine His dual nature. I am uncomfortable with the simple statement "Jesus is God," as if that's all there is to it. When we say that Jesus is God incarnate, that's a different matter; we are then saying that Christ is one person with two natures: human and divine. We do not believe in a deified human being; we do not believe that Jesus' human nature was divine. We believe that though Christ's divine nature is omniscient, His human nature was not. Thus, when Jesus draws on His human knowledge, there are certain things that He doesn't know. When Muslims take manifestations of the human nature of Jesus from the New Testament and use them to prove that Christ was not divine, it demonstrates their failure to understand the dual nature of Christ.

When the rich young ruler asks Jesus, "Good Teacher, what shall I do that I may inherit eternal life?" Jesus stops him in his tracks and says, "Why do you call Me good? No one is good but One, that is, God" (Mark 10:17-18). Some critics infer that Jesus is denying His goodness *and* His deity. However, if He *is* denying His goodness, He's also denying His own sinlessness, which would disqualify Him from offering an atonement. This inference flatly contradicts everything else Jesus said.

Let's examine what Jesus is saying here. The man who approached Him had no idea that he was talking to God incarnate, and he probably had a very superficial understanding of goodness. He may have thought that all teachers—or even all people—were basically good. Jesus could have replied, "Your problem, young man, is that you have no idea what goodness is." Instead of saying that, Jesus points him directly to the law, that standard by which we are shown to be less than good. He goes to the second table of the law. "You know the commandments: 'Do not commit adultery,' 'Do not murder,' 'Do not steal' . . ."

The man replies, "All these I have kept from my youth." He may have been thinking, "Is that all I have to do to get into heaven—keep the Ten Commandments?" Jesus could have said, "Obviously you weren't there when I gave the Sermon on the Mount, when I explained what the real demands are within these commandments, or you wouldn't make such a statement. You haven't kept any of these commandments since you got out of bed this morning."

Instead, Jesus may have thought, "Here's a rich man who thinks he has kept all the commandments. What's the first commandment? 'You shall have no other gods before me.' I'll give him a little test." So Jesus said, "Why don't you go sell all that you have, and give it to the poor, and follow me." And how did the man respond? He "went away sorrowful, for he had great possessions" (Mark 10:22). Thus Jesus, the masterful pedagogue, demonstrated that the man didn't begin to understand what goodness was, didn't begin to understand what the commandments required. Jesus is not saying here, "I am not good." Much to the contrary, He once asked His challengers, "Which of you convicts me of sin?" (John 8:46). Jesus identifies with sinlessness, not with sinfulness.

Muslims assert that Jesus Himself never claimed to be divine, that this claim was imposed on Him by the early church in their zeal to honor Him. Obviously, people today who say that Jesus never claimed to be divine fail to understand what His contemporaries understood: the thing that most infuriated the authorities of Christ's day was His claims to be divine. For example, when the Pharisees accused Jesus and His disciples of breaking the Sabbath, Jesus replied that "the Son of Man is Lord even of the Sabbath" (Matt. 12:8). Every Jew present understood the import of this statement—that the Sabbath day was instituted by God, and that only God has lordship over that creation ordinance. When Jesus claimed to be the Lord of the Sabbath, that was a claim to deity, and the crowd knew that.

Another example was Jesus' claim that He could forgive sins. The people responded, "Only God has the authority to forgive sins." He replied, "that you may know that the Son of Man has power on earth to forgive sins . . ." again claiming a divine prerogative (Matt. 9:6). In the Gospel of John, He often uses the Greek phrase *ego eimi,* as when He says, "I am the bread . . . I am the door . . . I am the good shepherd," and "Before Abraham was, I am" (John 6:35; 10:7, 14; 8:58). The divine formula of the ineffable name of God, Yahweh, was translated as *ego eimi* in the New Testament Greek. Thus, on multitudes of occasions Jesus consciously uses the language reserved exclusively for God in the Old Testament.

In these examples, when Jesus asserts His authority, He does not say directly, "That you may know that I have the power to forgive sins . . ." or "That you may know that I am the Lord of the Sabbath . . ." Rather, He says it somewhat cryptically: "the Son of Man is Lord even of the Sabbath." The most frequently used title for Jesus in the New Testament is *Christos,* or Christ, that is, "Messiah." "Jesus Christ" is not His name. His name is Jesus of Nazareth or Jesus bar Joseph. "Jesus" is His name; "Christ" is His title. Thus, when the New Testament says, "Jesus Christ," it is saying, "Jesus, Messiah."

The second most frequently given title for Jesus in the New

Testament is Lord, *kurios.* This is also the Old Testament title attributed to God. It is a divine title.

The third most frequently used title for Jesus in the New Testament—used eighty-two or eighty-three times—is "Son of Man." When Jesus referred to Himself, this is by far the title He most frequently used. In fact, of the eighty-two or eighty-three times this title is used in the New Testament, seventy-nine or eighty come from the lips of Jesus Himself. Oscar Cullman pointed out that if the early church community were writing a self-title back into the statements of Jesus, they would probably have instead used a title like "Lord" or "Messiah," rather than using the title "Son of Man." Thus, this is a clue that the biblical writers were being faithful to Jesus' own self-testimony.

The title Son of Man is a reference to an Old Testament concept—taken from Daniel 7—of a heavenly being, one who descends from heaven. Jesus Himself says, "No one has ascended to heaven but He who came down from heaven" (John 3:13). The descent from heaven is a concept central to New Testament Christology, which again puts Jesus on a far different plane from any apostle or any mere earthly prophet. Thus, the New Testament is replete with references to claims of Christ's heavenly origin.

Saleeb: Many Muslims don't understand the distinction between Jesus' human nature and His divine nature. When they hear someone say, "Jesus is God," they wonder, "If He is God, why is He praying to the Father?" And to whom was He praying on the cross when He said, "My God, My God . . ."

Sproul: That certainly underscores the importance of explaining that there are two distinct natures in this one person. When people try to combine Christ's two natures, as did the old Monophysite heresy that was condemned in the fifth century, it leads to the sorts of misunderstandings that we are discussing. In the example of Christ's words from the cross, it was the human nature of Jesus crying out. Christians must affirm not only the deity of Christ but also His full humanity.

Saleeb: The relationship between Jesus' humanity and His deity is not like the relationship between Clark Kent and Superman. Jesus wasn't just *pretending* to be human. He actually felt pain, He really felt hungry, and He truly died on the cross.

THE DARK SIDE OF ISLAM

Sproul: Abdul Saleeb and I trust that our readers have benefited by our discussion of the key points of conflict between Islam and Christianity. Unfortunately, the word "conflict" will remind many readers of another present reality: the rising tide of violence perpetrated in the name of Islam by Muslim individuals and organizations around the world. Is Islam a religion of peace or a religion of violence? I have asked Abdul to address this question from his unique perspective.

Saleeb: Since the terrorist attacks of September 11, 2001, many people have been asking questions about the issue of religion and violence. Many have started to wonder, "What is it in Islam that produces people who can engage in such horrible acts of terror and violence?" That is a legitimate question. As a former Muslim I am especially passionate about sharing answers to questions, especially with American Christians.

Let's focus on the issue of Islamic justification for violence and terrorism. My main thesis is very simple: the vast majority of Muslims are obviously very peaceful, fun-loving people who want a good future for themselves and their children. However, the minority of Muslims who are engaged in acts of terrorism do have religious justification for their actions based on the teachings of the Qur'an, the holy book of Islam, and based on examples from the prophet of Islam, Muhammad— his actions and his miscellaneous sayings and teachings that were later collected in other Islamic literature.

It is not true that Christians have always been nice and Muslims have not. Many atrocities have been committed throughout church history in the name of Christ. Muslims are fond of referring to the Crusades, the Inquisition, and the struggle in Northern Ireland between Protestants and Catholics. Christians have done and continue to do many evil things in the name of Jesus Christ; we need to confess these sins and repent of them. However, when Christians have engaged in such violence, they have betrayed the teachings of Jesus Christ and have turned their back on the examples that Christ set for us in the New Testament. But when Muslims engage in violence, murder, and other acts of terrorism, they can legiti- mately claim that they are following the commands of God as found in the Qur'an and in the examples of Muhammad and his teachings. This represents a major distinction between Christianity and Islam.

However, not all devout Muslims must necessarily become violent or become terrorists. There are many interpretations of the Qur'an, and many schools of thought in Islam, just as there are in Christianity and in most other religions. There are, for example, conservative Muslims and liberal Muslims as well as "Sufi" Muslims, who comprise the mystical wing of Islam. I grew up in a Sufi family. Sufis practice a sort of New Age version of Islam; they were just as horrified about the events of September 11 as you and I were.

Our understanding of violence in relation to Islam should not be limited to suicide bombings or planes blowing up buildings. The violence of Islam has taken many forms. The vast majority of cases of persecution of Christians around the world today occur in the Islamic world. For example, Christians in southern Sudan have been horribly persecuted for their faith by the Muslim government in northern Sudan. Another example of Islamic violence and aggression is the blasphemy law in Pakistan; it says that anyone who insults Muhammad commits a crime punishable by death. The roots of this law are in the earliest teachings of Islam itself. The Islamic law of apostasy states that any person who converts away from Islam to any other religion, whether that person becomes a Christian, a Jew, or whatever else, has committed a crime punishable by death.

Salman Rushdie is an Indian-born British author and a nominal Muslim. Some years ago, he wrote *The Satanic Verses,*[1] a novel in which he allegedly insulted Muhammad. The Ayatollah Khomeini, at that time the leader of the Islamic Republic of Iran, issued a *fatwa,* a religious ruling, that anyone who killed Rushdie would get a reward of several million dollars from the Iranian government.

Despite all these examples of Islamic violence, we keep hearing from various sources that Islam is a religion of love and peace. The week after September 11, for example, *Time*

magazine had a cover picture of Osama bin Laden. It also had
an article by Karen Armstrong entitled "The True Peaceful Face
of Islam." That same week *Newsweek* had an article entitled
"A Peaceful Faith, A Fanatic Few." The author wrote, "Islam:
even the sound of this lovely Arabic word, which means 'sur-
render,' conveys the promise of peace, justice, and harmony
that comes to those who do the will of God."[2]

Even our president has said that Islam is a religion of peace
and is a loving religion. Some claim that these violent Muslims
are to Islam what the Ku Klux Klan is to Christianity. Recently,
somebody made the claim that Osama bin Laden is to Islam
what Timothy McVeigh was to Christianity. These are
absolutely false analogies. Bin Laden can quote Qur'anic verses
and traditions from Muhammad that justify his actions.
McVeigh could not quote from the Bible or refer to Jesus to justify his actions. When the Klan commits acts of racial violence, they are betraying the teachings of Jesus Christ. These
false analogies and characterizations are being perpetuated by
Western media, politicians, and intellectuals.

Following September 11, the Muslim Council of Detroit
issued a statement saying that Muslim terrorists in general are
misinformed and misguided fanatics who are misinterpreting
Islamic texts. However, these terrorists, in fact, have many
texts from the Qur'an that they can correctly quote to support
the legitimacy of their actions of violence, terror, and persecution. Even though these Muslim terrorists might be few in
number compared with the 1.2 billion Muslims around the
world, nevertheless they represent a very serious issue that we
need to address.

Following are some of the Qur'anic verses that are used to support the Islamic violence we have described. All of these passages are supposedly direct revelations from God to Muhammad and the Muslim community.

"Fight in the cause of Allah those who fight you, . . . and slay them wherever you catch them, . . . and fight them on until there is no more tumult or oppression, and there prevail justice and faith in Allah" (Sura 2:190-193). The command is to keep fighting, to keep slaying wherever you catch the enemies of God.

In Sura 2:216, God says this to the Muslim community: "Fighting is prescribed upon you, and ye dislike it. But it is possible that ye dislike a thing which is good for you, and that ye love a thing which is bad for you. But Allah knoweth and ye know not." Here we see some reluctance on the part of the Muslim community to fight; but God tells them, "I know what is good for you."

Many verses in the Qur'an talk about the rewards of martyrdom. One of the basic messages is that if you die in the cause of God, that's your only sure way to heaven. "And if ye are slain, or die, in the way of Allah, forgiveness and mercy from Allah are far better than all they could amass. And if ye die, or are slain, lo! it is unto Allah that ye are brought together" (Sura 3:157-158). "Think not of those who are slain in Allah's way as dead. Nay, they live, finding their sustenance in the Presence of their Lord" (Sura 3:169). "Those who . . . have fought or been slain—verily, I will blot out from them their iniquities, and admit them into Gardens with rivers flowing beneath—a reward from the Presence of Allah" (Sura 3:195).

Numerous passages encourage violence against unbelievers, including Jews and Christians: "For the Unbelievers are unto you open enemies" (Sura 4:101). "They but wish that ye should reject Faith, as they do, and thus be on the same footing (as they): so take not friends from their ranks until they flee in the way of Allah. . . . But if they turn renegades, seize them and slay them wherever ye find them" (Sura 4:89). ". . . fight and slay the Pagans wherever you find them, and seize them, beleaguer them, and lie in wait for them in every stratagem (of war)" (Sura 9:5). "Fight those who believe not in Allah nor the Last Day, . . . nor acknowledge the Religion of Truth, from among the People of the Book [Jews and Christians]" (Sura 9:29).

Some of the violence commanded is particularly grue-some: "The punishment of those who wage war against Allah and His Messenger, and strive with might and main for mis-chief through the land is: execution, or crucifixion, or the cutting off of hands and feet from opposite sides, or exile from the land: that is their disgrace in this world, and a heavy punishment is theirs in the hereafter" (Sura 5:33). "Smite ye above their necks and smite all their fingertips off them. This because they contended against Allah and His Messenger. If any contend against Allah and His Messenger, Allah is strict in punishment" (Sura 8:12-13). "Therefore, when ye meet the Unbelievers (in fight), smite at their necks; at length, when ye have thoroughly subdued them, bind the bond firmly (on them)" (Sura 47:4).

Following is one of the verses that Osama bin Laden quoted in the videotape that the U.S. Army found in

Afghanistan. "Fight them, and Allah will punish them by your hands, cover them with shame" (Sura 9:14).

These are not isolated passages that some people are misinterpreting or quoting out of context. Such verses are prevalent throughout the Qur'an, supporting the view that Allah wants his people to fight and destroy the enemies of the people of Allah by the use of the sword and other violence. That destruction can take the form of assassinations, persecution, suicide bombings, or a death sentence on an author who supposedly ridicules the Islamic faith.

Many people today say that these verses were intended just for the time of Muhammad, when the pagans of Mecca were attacking him, and that they do not apply today. However, not even once in the entire Qur'an is there a restriction put on these verses. They simply tell Muslims to fight the unbelievers. And these verses have been used throughout fourteen hundred years of Islamic history to do exactly that. These verses continue to provide justification for Muslims killing or inflicting serious bodily harm on other Muslims and for Muslims killing "infidels," because the verses are universal for all time and all places.

In the Old Testament book of Joshua, God tells Joshua to destroy certain cities in the land of Canaan, but God specifically restricts His command to that time period for a special purpose and a specific people group. Nowhere in the later Old Testament period do we read general commands to fight the pagans and spread the monotheistic faith of the Jews.

Some Muslims are fond of saying that the *jihad*, or holy war, in Islam is only a defensive action. Only in cases of self-defense are Muslims allowed to fight; Muslims are never allowed to initiate a war. Diana Eck recently wrote a book entitled *A New Religious America,* which is about the growth of religions in America. In the chapter on Islam, she quotes Jamal Badawi, a famous Muslim professor and apologist. He claims that from a Muslim perspective, actual armed jihad is permissible under two conditions alone: for self-defense, or for fighting against oppression.[3] I agree.

However, he fails to point out that for many Muslims, "self-defense" and "fighting against oppression" have much broader meanings than you or I would associate with those terms. Muslims today have said that America is attacking them by exporting its secular cultural values, by exporting Hollywood movies and destroying the cultural norms of their countries. Thus they claim to be engaged in self-defense when they attack America.

Some Muslims call America "the great Satan"; thus, fighting America is fighting against oppression. The Ayatollah Khomeini used this argument to promote violence against Americans. Muslim terrorist groups such as Hamas and Hezbollah use a similar argument to attack Israeli civilians. Violence of this sort is not a recent phenomenon. Islam expanded phenomenally in the beginning of its history through acts of war. Muslims invaded the Persian Empire, North Africa, and Europe. None of the countries in those areas attacked Muslims first; Muslims were certainly not acting in self-defense. However, Islam has viewed as oppressive any government that does not allow Muslims to come in and set up Islam as a religion of the state. Therefore fighting against those governments is justified, because Islam is the true religion and fighting nonbelievers is equivalent to fighting against oppression.

The basic mentality of Islam is very simple. Muslims believe that God has sent prophets throughout history. Some of these prophets left revelations in books, but all of those books have been either lost or corrupted, except one: the book of the last prophet, Muhammad. His book, the Qur'an, is God's final, perfect, uncorrupted message to humanity. The mission of Islam is to take that message to the world.

Islam divides the world into two segments: the House of Islam and the House of War. The goal of Islam is to dominate the world: the House of Islam must conquer the House of War. In a sense, it is similar to the Great Commission of Jesus Christ: take the gospel to the end of the earth. The radical difference between the Great Commission of Jesus Christ and the mission of Islam is that Christians are not justified in using violence in spreading the message of Christ, but Muslims believe they are justified in using violence to spread their message.

Muslims do not believe only in the Qur'an as their ultimate source of authority. Some traditions and some sayings and actions of Muhammad are recorded in other books and incorporated into an authoritative body of teaching for Muslims.

In the second century of the Islamic era, Ibn Ishaq, a Muslim historian, wrote a biography of Muhammad titled *Sirat Rasul Allah*.[4] It includes descriptions of the pattern of violence in the life of Muhammad and the example that he sets for his followers in terms of violence.

Muhammad started his prophetic ministry when he was forty years old, in A.D. 610, when he believed that he began to receive revelations from God. For the first thirteen years he was basically a preacher in the city of Mecca. He preached messages about the oneness of God, the day of judgment, taking care of widows and orphans, and so on. His message was generally rejected by the pagan society. In the last ten years of his life he was invited to go to Medina, a city northeast of Mecca. He became the ruler of Medina. That's when he began to use violence, and Islam became highly political as it began to war against its enemies. When Muhammad first arrived in Medina, he encountered Jewish tribes living in its suburbs. Here is an excerpt from the constitution he wrote for the city: "A believer shall not slay a believer for the sake of an unbeliever, nor shall he aid an unbeliever against a believer. . . . Believers are friends one to the other to the exclusion of outsiders. . . . The believers must avenge the blood of one another shed in the way of God."[5]

Why was it so difficult for the United States to find Muslim allies for its coalition fighting in Afghanistan? Because Muhammad said, "Believers shall never join an unbeliever against another believer." Why are the Saudis and other Muslims upset that the U.S. Army is in Saudi Arabia? Because an infidel people are in their land. Believers and infidels should not be allies.

Muhammad ordered and orchestrated a series of assassinations against people who opposed him. The first person whom he had assassinated was an elderly Jewish man. Here is the account in Ishaq's biography of Muhammad: "The apostle said, . . . 'Who will rid me of Ibnu'l Ashraf?'" And then one of his followers volunteered, "I will deal with him for you, O apostle of God. I will kill him." The prophet gave him his blessing. Later the follower comes to Muhammad and tells him that in order to murder this man he would have to lie to him. Muhammad replies that lying is alright as long as you can kill this enemy. This follower and some other Muslims visit the man, entice him out of his house, attack him, and kill him with their daggers and swords. Then they report to the prophet that they have killed God's enemy. The author concludes this incident by writing, "Our attack upon God's enemy cast terror among the Jews, and there was no Jew in Medina who did not fear for his life."[6]

On the next page in the biography the author reports, "The Apostle said, 'Kill any Jew that falls into your power.'" He then tells the story of two brothers. The younger was a Muslim, the older was not. The Muslim brother kills a Jewish merchant. The other brother criticizes him, asking, "You enemy of God, did you kill him when much of the fat on your belly comes from his wealth?" In other words, "You did business with this man. Why did you kill him?" The younger brother, a devout Muslim, replied that he would have killed his brother, too, if Muhammad had ordered it. The older brother exclaimed, "By God, a religion that can bring you to this is marvelous!" And he became a Muslim.[7] This is an example of transformation through Islam. Compare this with our transformation in Christ!

Another story from this biography regards three Jewish tribes around the city of Medina. Muhammad had hoped that since they were monotheists these tribes would receive him as a prophet of God. However, they did not accept him or his prophetic calling. He responded by expelling the first two tribes. He orchestrated a series of events whereby a judgment was made against the third tribe: every man of that tribe would be beheaded, and the Muslims would take the women, the children, and the property. According to Islamic history, between 600 and 900 Jewish men were beheaded in that incident on the orders of Muhammad.

In another incident Muhammad and his army took over a town. They discovered that there were treasures hidden in the town. So they captured a man and brought him before Muhammad, telling him that the man knew where the treasure was hidden. The man refused to reveal the location to the prophet, who warned him, "We will kill you if you don't tell us." The man still refused to give up the information. According to the biography, "The apostle gave orders to al-Zubayr, 'Torture him until you extract what he has.' So he kindled a fire with flint and steel on his chest until he was nearly dead. Then the apostle delivered him to Muhammad b. Maslamah and he struck off his head."[8]

When his army conquered Mecca, Muhammad showed some restraint by not killing all his enemies. He tried to appease them by giving them gifts and buying their support. However, he did have several people killed simply because they had written poetry that ridiculed him.

On another occasion Muhammad ordered the death of his own uncle, Abu Sufyan, who was the leader of an opposition group. Some assassins went to Mecca to kill the uncle.

They failed and began their return to Medina. Along the way they encountered a one-eyed shepherd. According to the biography, the chief hired assassin said, as soon as the man was "asleep and snoring, I got up and killed him in a more horrible way than any man has been killed. I put the end of my bow in his sound eye. Then I bore down on it until I forced it out at the back of his neck. . . . When I got to Medina . . . the apostle asked my news and when I told him what had happened, he blessed me."[9]

The biography has accounts of other assassinations. Abu Afak showed his disaffection with Muhammad by composing a poem. Muhammad asked, "Who will deal with this rascal for me?" and one of his followers, Salim Umayr, killed Abu Afak.[10] After this assassination a woman named Asma displayed her disapproval and wrote a poem against Muhammad, criticizing him for his actions. "When the Apostle heard what she had said, he said 'Who will rid me of Marwan's daughter?' Umayr . . . who was with him heard him, and that very night he went to her house and killed her. In the morning he came to the apostle and told him what he had done, and he said, 'You have helped God and His Apostle, O Umayr.'"[11]

Some people today say that these are simply old Arab historians who loved gory details, and we can't fully trust those accounts. Muhammad Husayn Haykal, a twentieth-century Egyptian journalist, wrote a biography of Muhammad that is very popular in the Muslim world. He wanted to communicate the beauty of Muhammad's life and ministry to a Western audience. In his book he writes an account of this same assassination. Haykal describes how the old man went to assassinate this woman, but having poor eyesight, he groped for her as she was breast-feeding. He then grabbed the child and killed the mother. Astoundingly, Haykal doesn't try to provide any justi-fication or explanation for the Western audience reading this account. Instead, he tells how the woman's relatives confronted Umayr and he said that he would kill them too if they per-sisted in challenging his actions. Haykal writes that the woman's relatives were emboldened in their Islamic faith because of the courage of that assassin.[12] Thus, this twentieth-century Egyptian intellectual considers the killing of a woman as she is breast-feeding her child a courageous act. Haykal does not even question the moral aspects of this kind of an assassi-nation. He simply goes on to describe another assassination.

Besides the actions of Muhammad, another important thing that has shaped the Islamic legal system is the collection of Muhammad's sayings, the Hadith. The most ancient version is by al-Bukhari. In Sunni Islam this book is second in impor-tance only to the Qur'an. The English translation is a nine-volume set with Arabic on one side and English on the other side. I will mostly quote from al-Bukhari some of the sayings of Muhammad:

"Allah's apostle said, 'Know that paradise is under the shades of swords.'"[13]

Elsewhere: "Allah's apostle said, 'I have been ordered to fight with the people till they say, "None has the right to be worshipped but Allah," and whoever says, "None has the right to be worshipped but Allah," his life and property will be saved by me.'"[14]

Another saying, particularly disturbing: "It is not fitting for a prophet that he should have prisoners of war [and free them with ransom] until he has made a great slaughter [among his enemies] in the land."[15]

The following saying is the basis of the law of apostasy in Islam: "Whoever changed his Islamic religion, then kill him."[16]

These sayings also describe an incident of Muhammad killing someone who was a spy in his camp. On another occasion, some people came to Muhammad asking for help. After he helped them, they killed one of his followers and ran away. The prophet ordered them to be arrested. When they were brought back to him, Muhammad ordered that their hands and legs were to be cut off, their eyes were to be branded with heated pieces of iron, and the stumps of their severed hands and legs were to be cauterized till they were dead.

In another incident, "The Prophet passed by me at a place called al-Abwah or Waddan, and was asked whether it was permissible to attack the pagan warriors at night with the probability of exposing their women and children to danger. The Prophet replied, 'They [the women and children] are from them [pagans].'"[17]

A man named "Muslim" also has compiled an authoritative collection of many of the traditions of Muhammad. He discusses the above saying of Muhammad in a chapter about the permissibility of killing women and children in night raids, provided their killing is not deliberate. He writes, "It is reported . . . that the Prophet of Allah (may peace be upon him), when asked about the women and children of the polytheists being killed during the night raid, said: They are from them."[18] In other words, "It is all right to kill them."

Another series of traditions from Muhammad was collected by Abu Dawud. One of the chapters is entitled "Excellence of Killing an Infidel." It relates this saying: "Abu Harairah reported the Apostle of Allah (may peace be upon him) as saying: An infidel and the one who killed him will never be brought together in Hell." The Muslim translator of this work adds the following footnote to this tradition: "This means that a person who kills an infidel while fighting in Allah's path will have his sins remitted and forgiven, and will, therefore, go to Paradise. The infidel will inevitably go to Hell. Thus the man who killed an infidel will not be brought together in Hell with him."[19]

Another chapter in this collection is entitled "Punishment of a Man Who Abuses the Prophet." The author recounts the story of a Muslim man who killed a woman who was both his slave and his concubine. They had two children together. He stabbed her to death because she had disparaged Muhammad. The next day he was afraid that he might be punished for killing the woman, but he told the prophet, "I killed this woman because she was disparaging you." Muhammad replied, "O, be witness, no retaliation is payable for her blood."[20]

The next incident in this chapter is reported by another Muslim leader. He said that a Jewess had abused the prophet and disparaged him. A man strangled her till she died. Muhammad declared that no recompense was payable for her blood. The translator of this tradition writes in the footnotes: "It is unanimously agreed that if a Muslim abuses or insults the Prophet . . . he should be killed. . . . even if a Jew or any non-Muslim abuses the Prophet . . . he will be killed."[21]

Thus, anything that is said against the prophet of Islam can be viewed as an insult and as a crime punishable by death. In fact, this is the law in the country of Pakistan. As we have seen, violence in Islam has taken many forms, such as the persecution of minorities, the killing of political and religious opponents, and acts of terrorism. And all of these actions find their roots in the Qur'an and in the actions and sayings of Muhammad.

What I have been relating are not simply ancient sayings that are no longer relevant today. Recently PBS, not a bastion of conservative reporting, broadcast an edition of *Frontline* called "The Saudi Time Bomb." It described the rise of religious fundamentalism in Saudi Arabia and how the oil money there is supporting this fundamentalism and exporting it all over the Muslim world. The program's website had a segment about education in that country, 35 percent of which is mandatory religious education. One of the mandatory textbooks used today is a collection of Muhammad's sayings, many of which I discussed earlier. One of these sayings is entitled "The Victory of Muslims over Jews." This is taught to junior high students in Saudi Arabia today.

Unfortunately, evangelical Christians are guilty of sin with regard to Muslims: racism, prejudice, and fear. We are already separated from our Muslim neighbors, colleagues, and coworkers because we are afraid of them. I don't want to say anything that would add to that fear and would make anyone move even farther away from them. My purpose in sharing this material has not been to call for a crusade against Islam. The purpose for sharing this material is for you to be aware of the religious roots of violence in Islam and to take this background more seriously. My ultimate goal is to take us to the cross and ask Christ for the strength and courage to witness to our Muslim friends, colaborers, colleagues, and neighbors—to witness to them with greater boldness and love and humility.

NOTES

INTRODUCTION

1. Norman L. Geisler and Abdul Saleeb, *Answering Islam: The Crescent in Light of the Cross* (Grand Rapids, Mich.: Baker, 2002).
2. Immanuel Kant, quoted in *Christopher Hall*, "Adding Up the Trinity," *Christianity Today*, April 28, 1997, 26.
3. Thomas Jefferson, quoted in ibid.
4. Dorothy L. Sayers, "The Dogma Is the Drama," in *The Whimsical Christian: Eighteen Essays by Dorothy L. Sayers* (New York: Collier, 1987), 25.
5. C. Stephen Evans, *The Historical Christ and the Jesus of Faith* (New York: Oxford University Press, 1996), 17.
6. All three magazines published their stories on April 8, 1996.

CHAPTER 1:
ISLAM AND CHRISTIANITY ON SCRIPTURE

1. All quotations from the Qur'an are taken from Abdullah Yusuf Ali, *The Holy Qur'an: Text, Translation, and Commentary*, New Revised Edition (Brentwood, Md.: Amana Corporation, 1989).
2. Emil Brunner, *Der Mittler* (1927; translated as *The Mediator*, trans. Olive Wyon [Philadelphia: Westminster, 1947]).

CHAPTER 2:
ISLAM AND CHRISTIANITY ON THE FATHERHOOD OF GOD

1. Abdullah Yusuf Ali, *The Holy Qur'an: Text, Translation, and Commentary*, New Revised Edition (Brentwood, Md.: Amana Corporation, 1989), 751.
2. Ibid., 49.
3. Ibid.
4. Adolf von Harnack, *What Is Christianity?* (New York: Harper, 1957).

CHAPTER 3:
ISLAM AND CHRISTIANITY ON THE TRINITY

1. Shabbir Akhtar, *A Faith for All Seasons: Islam and the Challenge of the Modern World* (Chicago: Ivan R. Dee, 1991), 179.
2. Ibid.
3. C. S. Lewis, *Mere Christianity* (New York: Macmillan, 1960), 142.

CHAPTER 4:
ISLAM AND CHRISTIANITY ON SIN

1. Shabbir Akhtar, *A Faith for All Seasons: Islam and the Challenge of the Modern World* (Chicago: Ivan R. Dee, 1991), 155.
2. Isma'il al-Faruqi, *Islam* (Niles, Ill.: Argus, 1984), 9.

CHAPTER 5:
ISLAM AND CHRISTIANITY ON SALVATION

1. Isma'il al-Faruqi, "On the Nature of Islamic Da'wah." *Evangelical Review of Theology* 20 [1996]: 134-135.
2. Ibid., 135.
3. Badru D. Kateregga, in Badru D. Kateregga and David W. Shenk, *Islam and Christianity: A Muslim and a Christian in Dialogue* (Grand Rapids, Mich.: Eerdmans, 1981), 175.
4. R. C. Sproul, *The Holiness of God* (Wheaton, Ill.: Tyndale, 2000).
5. Isma'il al-Faruqi, *Islam* (Niles, Ill.: Argus, 1984), 5.

CHAPTER 6:
ISLAM AND CHRISTIANITY ON THE DEATH OF CHRIST

1. Kenneth Cragg, quoted in Evertt W. Huffard, "Culturally Relevant Themes About Christ," in J. Dudley Woodberry, ed., *Muslims and Christians on the Emmaus Road* (Monrovia, Calif.: MARC, 1989), 165.

CHAPTER 7:
ISLAM AND CHRISTIANITY ON THE DEITY OF CHRIST

1. Misha'al ibn Abdullah, *What Did Jesus Really Say?* (Ann Arbor, Mich.: Islamic Assembly of North America, 1996).
2. Robert W. Funk, Roy W. Hoover, and The Jesus Seminar, *The Five Gospels: What Did Jesus Really Say?* (New York: Free Press, 1993).
3. John Hick, ed., *The Myth of God Incarnate* (Philadelphia: Westminster, 1977).

CHAPTER 8:
THE DARK SIDE OF ISLAM

1. Salman Rushdie, *The Satanic Verses* (New York: Viking, 1988).
2. Kenneth L. Woodward, "A Peaceful Faith, A Fanatic Few," *Newsweek,* September 24, 2001, 67-68.
3. Diana L. Eck, *A New Religious America:* (San Francisco: HarperSanFrancisco, 2001), 238.
4. Translated as Ibn Ishaq, *The Life of Muhammad: A Translation of Ishaq's Sirat Rasul Allah,* trans. A. Guillaume (New York: Oxford University Press, 1955).
5. Ibid., 232.
6. Ibid., 367-368.
7. Ibid., 369.
8. Ibid., 515.
9. Ibid., 674-675.
10. Ibid., 675.
11. Ibid., 676.
12. Muhammad Husayn Haykal, *The Life of Muhammad,* trans. Isma'il al-Faruqi (Indianapolis: North American Trust Publications, 1976), 243.
13. Al-Bukhari, *The Translation of the Meanings of Sahih Al-Bukhari,* trans. Muhammad Muhsin Khan, 9 vols. (Al-Medina: Islamic University, n.d.), 4:55.
14. Ibid., 4:124.
15. Ibid., 4:161.
16. Ibid., 9:45.
17. Ibid., 4:158-159.
18. *Sahih Muslim,* trans. Abdul Hamid Siddiqi, 4 vols (Chicago: Kazi, 1994), 3:946-947.
19. Abu Dawud, *Sunan Abu Dawud,* trans. Ahmad Hasan, 3 vols. (New Delhi: Kitab Bhavan, 1990), 2:690.
20. Ibid., 3:1214-1215.
21. Ibid., 3:1215.

GENERAL INDEX

Abdullah, Misha'al ibn, 74
Abraham, 30
Adam, 45
    as first prophet, 46
    effect of, 11, 46-47, 49, 53
Akhtar, Shabbir, 37-38, 46
Albright, William Foxwell, 20
al-Faruqi, Isma'il, 47, 56, 63
Ali, Abdullah Yusuf, 26-27
America
    as infidels, 92
    as "the great Satan," 90
    Muslims in, 8
Amos, 59
Aristotle, 38
atonement, 11-12, 52, 64, 70-71
Augustinian school, 48

Badawi, Jamal, 90
"Be all that you can be" slogan, 47
Belshazzar, 59
bin Laden, Osama, 86, 88
Brunner, Emil, 19
Bush, George W., 86

Calvin, John, 51
Camus, Albert, 58
Christians
    as family of God, 31-32
    definition of, 48
    persecution of, 85

sins of, 84, 99
comparative religion, 28
contradiction, 38-41
creation, 45-46
crucifixion
    Islamic denial of, 9, 66-67
    Qur'anic denial of, 66
Cullman, Oscar, 80

David, 31-32, 53, 59
Dawud, Abu, 98
Docetism, 39

Eck, Diana, 90
Edwards, Jonathan, 49-50
Evans, C. Stephen, 11
evolutionary philosophy, 20

fatherhood of God, 8-9
    as Christian intimacy, 9, 30
    as common address, 29-30
    as Islamic blasphemy, 25, 27
    as universal, 27-28
    not of sexual nature, 26-27
    title of Father, 29
Finney, Charles, 49
Fuller Seminary, 33, 57

God
    adoption by, 31
    as begetter, 26

SCRIPTURE INDEX

Qur'anic References Index